THE WRITINGS OF ANNA FREUD
Volume I

INTRODUCTION TO PSYCHOANALYSIS

Lectures for Child Analysts and Teachers

1922–1935

THE WRITINGS OF ANNA FREUD

Volume I

INTRODUCTION TO PSYCHOANALYSIS

Lectures for Child Analysts and Teachers

1922–1935

INTERNATIONAL UNIVERSITIES PRESS, INC.

NEW YORK

Library of Congress Cataloging in Publication Data

Freud, Anna 1895–
    Introduction to psychoanalysis (1922–1935)

    (The writings of Anna Freud, v. 1)
    Includes bibliographical references.
    1. Psychoanalysis. 2. Child analysis. I. Title.
[DNLM: 1. Psychoanalysis. 2. Psychoanalysis—In infancy and childhood. WM460 F887 in 1973]
BF721.F692 vol. 1   [BF173]   618.9′28′908s   [618.9′28′917]
ISBN 0–8236–6870–3   73–16853

Manufactured in the United States of America

Contents

Part III

Early Papers

Introduction

Since the 1920s, when the books and papers contained in this Volume were written, some dramatic changes have taken place in the whole field of work with children. Child analysis is no longer a pioneering venture needing to establish its right of existence even in the psychoanalytic world. The application of psychoanalytic knowledge to the upbringing of children has become a more or less accepted fact and has found its way, in many disguises, into the training programs for teachers and child care workers. To ascribe to the nature of children sexual as well as aggressive impulses has ceased to be an offense against the formerly cherished belief in the innocence of childhood. On the contrary, the slow and laborious steps of development which have to be taken by children before they can reach maturity and adapt to a civilized community are by now appreciated, so that children may find help and sympathy where previously they would have met with criticism and condemnation.

This change in outlook, which is almost worldwide, is

the result of the efforts of many individual people, within and also outside the psychoanalytic world. The Bibliography appended to this book attempts to pay at least partial tribute to the former.

In Vienna, from 1927 onward, a group of analysts, later joined by colleagues from Budapest and Prague, held regular meetings with me to discuss the child-analytic technique I had suggested, to report on cases treated with this method, to compare results, and to clarify the theoretical background of our clinical findings. If, in the beginning, the age range of children treated had been restricted to the latency period, this was soon extended downward to age 2 and upward to early and late adolescence. Children with all types of nonorganic disturbances of development were taken into treatment—from those with the usual phobias, hysterical illnesses, obsessional disturbances, bed wetting, stammering, compulsive masturbation, exhibitionism, and neurotic constipation to those with grave abnormalities of a borderline or schizophrenic type. Analyses of delinquent children were attempted and carried out in close cooperation with August Aichhorn, who developed and taught his approach to "wayward children" in Vienna at the same time.

Apart from these therapeutic developments, Vienna had at that time also become a fertile ground for the analytic study of normal child development and for the application of these new findings to education. Many of us had for years been listening to the inspiring lectures for teachers and youth leaders given by Siegfried Bernfeld, and many young and enthusiastic workers had joined his educational experiment in "Kinderheim Baumgarten," a camp school for children made homeless by World War I. Thus, the

Four Lectures for Teachers and Parents contained in this Volume were not an independent venture of mine but were commissioned by the Board of Education of the City of Vienna, and were furthermore followed by a regular seminar for nursery school teachers conducted by Dorothy Burlingham and myself. By this time, several members of the Vienna Psychoanalytic Society devoted a fair share of their teaching and lecturing activity to consolidating the ground which had been gained. A child guidance clinic for young children was directed by Editha Sterba, a similar clinic for adolescents by August Aichhorn. Dr. W. Hoffer initiated a three-year postgraduate training course for teachers, and also edited the first Journal of Psychoanalytic Education. To these ventures was added in 1937 an experimental day nursery for toddlers, founded and maintained by Dr. Edith Jackson, and administered by myself in conjunction with Dorothy Burlingham and the pediatrician Dr. Josephine Stross.

Promising as these undertakings seemed at the time, they came to a natural end when Hitler invaded Austria in 1938. This meant not a cessation of the work itself, but rather the emigration and spread of numerous analytically trained workers to other countries and continents, foremost to England and the United States. So far as the British Psycho-Analytical Society was concerned, our "continental" brand of child analysis was not readily accepted by its members. In the intervening years, and concurrently with our Viennese efforts, Melanie Klein had initiated and developed a different type of analysis for children, based in large part on an independent, new theory of early child development. This led to many controversies over the years, technical as well as theoretical. It also led to a delay of the publication of my *Four Lectures on Child Analysis*, which did not appear in English until the end of World War II.

World War II prompted us in England to create a direct heir to the Jackson Nursery in Vienna, i.e., the much enlarged, residential war nurseries, known under the name of "Hampstead Nurseries" where more than 80 war babies and young children were housed from 1939–1945 and, incidentally, provided an unprecedented and unending source of observational material for all of us who shared in the care of them. Records of these observations are laid down in the Monthly Reports to the Foster Parents' Plan for War Children, Inc., who financed this expensive undertaking. These were published in full in Volume III of the present series with the intention of offering the reader a detailed view of attempts at a psychoanalytically inspired upbringing of infants and young children, so far as this was feasible under the adverse conditions of a worldwide war. The Monthly Reports, filled as they are with accounts of coping with practical difficulties, shortages, and threats from enemy action, lay no claim to scientific value. What proved of value nevertheless were the conclusions drawn by us concerning a number of topics that have vital relevance to normal and abnormal child development: the effect of separation of infant and mother at a time when the biological unity between the two partners is at its height; a comparison between developmental progression under family and residential conditions; the reactions of toddlers to community life in which the relationship to peers takes the place of the normal ties to parents or other adults in parental roles; the oedipal development in the absence of oedipal objects, especially fathers.

With the return of peace conditions, and after the

Hampstead Child-Therapy Course and Clinic had taken the place of the Hampstead Nurseries, therapeutic child analysis and an intensive form of training for it came into their own once more. Maintaining the balance between clinical and applied psychoanalytic work, the further volumes in this series give evidence of my spread of interest from pathology to normality in childhood; to careful assessment of the various developmental stages and their dependence on the interaction between the appropriate environmental and internal factors; to diagnostic statements based on metapsychological assessments of the immature personality; to a schema of diagnostic categories that are divorced from adult psychopathology and linked exclusively to the degree of deviation from the expected norm in childhood. While many of these subjects are treated in detail in Volume VI, Volumes IV, V, and VII venture further and explore the problems of indication and contraindication for child analysis; the knotty problems of analytic training for work in the child as well as in the adult field; the possibility of actually carrying out scientifically valid research in psychoanalysis in the absence of laboratory conditions, quantification of results, the setting up of control groups, and other limitations.

If I now look back to my first book from the vantage point of almost a half century of psychoanalytic experience, I can only repeat here what I have affirmed on other occasions,[1] namely, that a number of statements made in

[1] For example, in my 1946 Preface to *The Psychoanalytical Treatment of Children.* This Preface has been omitted from this Volume to make way for an "Introduction" to serve the seven Volumes of my Writings. Nevertheless, its essential elements have been incorporated here.

my *Four Lectures on Child Analysis* in 1926 have to be modified. It is no longer true that child analysts work in a psychological vacuum and cannot trust either parents or teachers to supplement their analytic efforts with the necessary educational and supporting ones. The latter burden which in earlier years used to fall on the therapist can now be shared with the child's environment in most instances. Similarly, it is much easier than it used to be for the child analysts to gain entrance into the child's hidden internal world. What used to be effected by a prolonged introductory or preparatory phase to the treatment proper is now almost invariably brought about by the scrutiny and analysis of the patient's defensive mechanisms and maneuvers.

Both these changes, the one with regard to the child analyst's nonanalytic role, the other with regard to the abandonment of an introductory period, have had their impact on a further point which since 1926 has been the subject of much controversy, i.e., the presence or absence of true transference phenomena in child analysis. I now agree fully that during analytic treatment children regard their analyst not only as a new object for their affectionate or hostile, sexual or aggressive impulses, or as a helping person with whom they can establish a working alliance, but that, with therapy conducted within the correct limits, multitudes of transference phenomena appear, either additional to or instead of the same impulses and behavioral attitudes that the child displayed toward his original objects. I cannot say the same of my convictions concerning the full-blown transference neurosis as we expect it to develop in adult neurotics who undergo psychoanalytic treatment in its classic form. I believe that in child analysis it is extremely rare that we see the original neurotic formations linked with the parents disappear altogether to be replaced by new symptoms centered exclusively around the person of the analyst.

As regards the rest of the material in Volume I, I was content to present it as originally published, with the exception that I have entirely revised the original English translations. There are many basic views which have remained the same for me, even though, as shown in the later Volumes, they needed and received more detailed elaboration and additions and led to a large number of further applications.

Acknowledgments

Since much of my work published in these seven volumes was based on clinical impressions gained in the various departments of the Hampstead War Nurseries and the Hampstead Child-Therapy Course and Clinic, especially those starting with Volume III, I want to take this occasion to express my gratitude to the many individuals and organizations that have so generously supported these institutions over many years.

I owe a great debt for the grants and contributions received from:

American Philanthropic Foundation, New York
Gustave M. Berne Foundation, New York
Lionel Blitsten Memorial, Chicago
G. G. Bunzl Fund, London
H. Daroff Foundation, New York
Division Fund, Chicago
Field Foundation, New York
Ford Foundation, New York

Foster Parents' Plan for War Children, New York

Foundation for Research in Psychoanalysis, Beverly Hills, California

Foundations' Fund for Research in Psychiatry, New Haven, Connecticut

Anna Freud Foundation, New York

Freud Centenary Fund, London

Grant Foundation, New York

Floria Haas Estate, New York

Lita A. Hazen Charitable Trust, Radnor, Pennsylvania

A. and M. Lasker Foundation, New York

Andrew W. Mellon Fund, New York

Walter E. Meyer Research Institute of Law, New York

National Institute of Mental Health, Bethesda, Maryland

New-Land Foundation, New York

Norman Foundation, New York

Old Dominion Foundation, New York

Overbrook Fund, New York

Psychoanalytic Fund for Research and Development, New York

William Rosenwald Family Fund, New York

William Sachs Foundation, New York

W. Clement and Jessie V. Stone Foundation, Chicago

Taconic Foundation, New York

Publishing History

New York & Washington: Nervous and Mental Disease Publishing Company.

1946 [As Parts I & II in:] *The Psycho-Analytic Treatment of Children*. London: Imago Publishing Co.

1959 New York: International Universities Press.

1964 New York: Schocken Books.

French

1930– Introduction à la psychanalyse des enfants. *Revue*
1932 *Française de Psychanalyse*, 4:428–439, 610–633; 5:71–96.

1969 *Le Traitement psychanalytique des Enfants*. Paris: Presses Universitaires de France.

Danish

1948 *Psykoanalitisk behandling af børn*. Copenhagen: Munksgaards Boghandel.

Dutch

1950 *De psychoanalytische Behandeling van Kindern*. Amsterdam: De Spieghel.

Italian

1954 *Psicoanalisi e Bambini*. Milan: Mondadori Editore.
1972 *Il Trattamento Psicoanalitico dei Bambini*. Torino: Editore Boringhieri.

Japanese

1962 Tokyo: Seishin Shobo Co.

Spanish

1964   *Psicoanálisis del Niño.* Buenos Aires: Editorial Hormé.

Portuguese

1971   *O tratamento psicanalitico de criancas.* Rio de Janeiro: Imago.

PART II

FOUR LECTURES ON PSYCHOANALYSIS FOR TEACHERS AND PARENTS

German

1929   [Lecture 4] Die Beziehung zwischen Psychoanalyse und Pädagogik. *Zeitschrift für psychoanalytische Pädagogik,* 3:445–454.

1930   *Einführung in die Psychoanalyse für Pädagogen: Vier Vorträge.* Stuttgart: Hippokrates.

1935   [As Volume 8 of *Bücher des Werdens*] Bern: Hans Huber Verlag.

1956   [revised] Bern: Hans Huber Verlag.

English

1931   *Introduction to Psycho-Analysis for Teachers: Four Lectures.* London: Allen & Unwin.

1935   *Psychoanalysis for Teachers and Parents.* New York: Emerson Books.

1960   Boston: Beacon Press.

Dutch

1932   *Inleiding in de Psycho-Analyse voor Paedagogen.*
The Hague: N. V. Boekhandel en Uitgevers-Mijh
v. h. W. P. Van Stockum & Zoon.

Italian

1935   *Psicoanalisi per gli educatori.* Rome: Paolo Cremonese Editore.

Spanish

1946   *Introduccion al psicoanálisis para educadores.* Buenos Aires: Paidos.

Sinhalese

1956   Ceylon: Guanesana.

Japanese

1963   Toyko: Seishin Shobo.

French

1968   *Initiation à la psychanalyse pour educateurs.* Toulouse: E. Privat.

Part I

FOUR LECTURES ON CHILD
ANALYSIS (1927 [1926])

See Publishing History (pp. xviiff.) for previous publications.
The version presented here has been revised by the author.

LECTURE 1

Preparation for Child
Analysis

Ladies and Gentlemen: I find it difficult to say anything about the technique of child analysis without approaching first the general question in which cases I would consider the analysis of a child to be indicated and in which cases I would think it preferable to refrain from undertaking it.[1]

Melanie Klein in Berlin (1923, 1926) has, as is well known, fully discussed this problem in her publications and lectures. She takes the view that any disturbance in the intellectual or emotional development of a child can be resolved or at least favorably influenced by an analysis. She

[1] See the author's later discussion of indications and contraindications in *Writings*, Vol. IV ch. 1; Vol. VI, ch. 6; Vol. VII, ch. 8.

3

goes still further in maintaining that an analysis also greatly benefits the development of any normal child and will in the course of time become an indispensable complement to all modern upbringing. In contrast to this, a discussion in the Vienna Psychoanalytic Society last year showed that the majority of our members think differently, and maintain that analysis is appropriate only where a child has developed a genuine infantile neurosis.

I am afraid that in the course of these lectures I shall not be able to contribute much to the elucidation of this question. The most I can do is to report to you in which cases I have undertaken an analysis, in which of them this decision proved justified, and in which the analysis came to grief owing to internal or external difficulties. Recent successes as well as recent failures inevitably play their part when new assessments and decisions have to be approached. On the whole, I think that in working with children sometimes the impression is given that analysis as a method is too difficult, costly, and cumbersome to be employed, that it tries to do too much; in other cases—and these are more frequent—the feeling emerges that analysis proper accomplishes too little.

Thus, it may turn out that analysis, where children are concerned, requires certain modifications and adjustments, or indeed can be undertaken only subject to specific precautions. Where it is technically not feasible to observe these precautions, it may be inadvisable to attempt analysis.

In the course of these lectures specific examples will be used to clarify and illustrate the foregoing assertions. Leaving them deliberately aside for the present, I turn first to the technique of child analysis in those cases where for some reason or other it seems advisable to undertake that treatment.

Until now I have always refrained from reporting on the analysis of a child, and from examining in that connection the special technique of child analysis, since I was afraid that anything to be said on this subject would seem too obvious. The technique of child analysis, insofar as it is special at all, derives from one very simple fact: that the adult is—at least to a considerable degree—a mature and independent being, while the child is immature and dependent. It is evident that to deal with such different subjects the method cannot remain the same. Many of its elements, important and significant in an adult case, lose their importance in the new situation; the roles played by various auxiliary procedures change: what is necessary for the adult may be risky for the child. It is well known that in adult cases too, there are circumstances which call for modifications of technique; this hardly requires special theoretical explanations.

However, in the last two and a half years, I had the opportunity to conduct ten long analyses of children which led to a number of worthwhile observations. In what follows I shall try to present these, keeping aware of the fact that, given the same material, anybody in the audience would have arrived at similar impressions.

Keeping to the actual sequence of events as they occurred in the analyses, I begin with the attitude of the child at the beginning of the analytic work.

Let us consider first the analogous situation with an adult patient. A person feels that he is disturbed, in his work or his enjoyment of life, by some sort of difficulty within himself; he gains, for one reason or another, confidence in the therapeutic power of analysis or in some particular analyst; and he makes the decision to seek a remedy by this means. I know of course that the facts are not always altogether like this. It is not always exclusively the inner difficulties which are the motive for the analysis—frequently the professed motives are conflicts with the environment which have been induced by the inner difficulties. Further, the decision is not always made wholly independently; pressure from relatives or others often plays a role greater than is favorable for the progress of the subsequent analytic work. Nor is confidence in analysis and the analyst always a factor. Nevertheless, from a therapeutic point of view, we regard it as the desirable and ideal situation that the patient of his own free will allies himself with the analyst against a part of his own inner being.

This state of affairs is of course never found in children. The decision to seek analysis is never made by the child patient but always by the parents or other persons responsible for him. The child is not asked for his consent. If the question were put to him, he could hardly pronounce an opinion or find an answer. The analyst is a stranger, analysis itself something unknown.

What constitutes an even greater difficulty, however, is that in many cases the child himself does not suffer, for he is often not aware of any disturbances in himself; only the environment suffers from his symptoms or aggressive outbursts. Thus, the situation lacks everything which seems indispensable in the case of the adult: insight into illness, voluntary decision, and the wish to be cured.

This does not impress every analyst of children as a serious obstacle. Melanie Klein, in the writings mentioned before, describes how she comes to terms with these circumstances and what technique she bases on them. To me, on the other hand, it seems worth exploring whether with children it may not be possible to bring about the same attitudes which have proved so favorable in the case of adults, i.e., whether one cannot in some way produce in the child the missing willingness to undergo analysis.

This first lecture, in fact, is meant to demonstrate how in six different cases of children, between the ages of 6 to 11, I succeeded in making the small patient "analyzable" in the sense in which we would say that an adult is analyzable; in other words, how I induced in the child insight into his disturbance, imparted confidence in the analyst, and turned the decision for analysis from one taken by others into his own. To accomplish this task, I thought that child analysis required a preparatory period, one which does not occur with adults.

I emphasize that everything undertaken in this period still is far removed from real analytic work; that is to say, there is as yet no question of making unconscious processes conscious or of analyzing transferences and resistances. It is simply a matter of converting an unsuitable situation into a desirable one, by all the means which are at the disposal of an adult dealing with a child.

This period of preparation—a period of "breaking the child in" for analysis, one might call it—will vary according to the degree to which the situation of an individual child differs from that which we deem the ideal one in the case of adults. The further the child's state is from this desirable condition, the longer the preparatory period will last.

Such a task need not always be difficult since the step to

be taken is often not a very big one. I am reminded of the case of a little 6-year-old girl who was sent to me last year for three weeks' observation. I had to determine whether the difficult, silent, and unpleasing nature of the child was due to a defective disposition and unsatisfactory intellectual development, or whether we had here a case of an especially inhibited, dreamy, and withdrawn child. Closer observation revealed the presence of an obsessional neurosis, unusually severe and well-defined for such an early age, together with acute intelligence and keen logical powers.

In this case the introductory process proved very simple. The little girl already knew two children who were being analyzed by me, and she came to her first appointment with her slightly older friend. I said nothing special to her, and merely let her become familiar with the strange surroundings.

The next time, when I had her alone, I made the first approach. I said that she knew quite well why her two friends came to me: one because he could never tell the truth and wanted to give up this habit, and the other because she cried so often and was angry with herself for doing so; and I wondered whether she too had been sent to me for some such reason. Whereupon she said quite straightforwardly, "I have a devil in me. Can it be taken out?"

I was for a moment taken aback at this unexpected answer. Certainly it could, I said, but it would be no light work. And if I were to try with her to do it, she would have to do a lot of things which she would not find at all agreeable. (I meant, of course, that she would have to tell me everything no matter how unpleasant.)

She became quite serious and thoughtful before she replied, "If you tell me that this is the only way to do it, and to do it quickly, then I shall do it that way." Thereby of her own free will she bound herself to the fundamental analytic rule. We ask nothing more of an adult patient at the outset. But further, she fully understood that a lengthy time period would be required.

When the three trial weeks were up her parents were undecided whether to leave her in analysis with me or to make other provisions for her care. She herself, however, was very disquieted, did not want to give up the hope I had awakened that she could be cured, and insistently demanded that, even if she had to leave me, I should rid her of her devil in the remaining three or four days.

I assured her that this was impossible and that it would take a long time of working together. I could not make this intelligible to her in the usual way, for although she was of school age, she had as yet no knowledge of numbers on account of her numerous inhibitions. Thereupon she sat herself down on the floor, pointed at the pattern of my oriental rug, and said, "Will it take as many days as there are red bits? Or even as the green bits?" I showed her the great number of appointments that would be necessary by referring to the many medallions in the pattern. She fully grasped the point, and in the imminent decision did her part in persuading her parents of the necessity for a very long time of working with me.

You may say that in this case it was the severity of the neurosis itself which lightened the work of the analyst. But I think that would be an error. I will quote another case in which the introductory phase took a similar course, although there a neurosis proper was not in evidence at all.

About two and a half years ago I made the analytic acquaintance of an 11-year-old girl whose upbringing had caused great difficulties in her home. She came from a well-to-do middle-class family, with the conditions in her home far from favorable. Her father was weak and little concerned with her, her mother had been dead for some years, and her relationships with the father's second wife and a younger stepbrother were troubled. A number of thefts by the child, and an unending series of crude lies and minor and major concealments and insincerities had induced the stepmother, on the advice of the family physician, to seek the aid of analysis. Here the analytic treaty was equally simple. "Your parents cannot do anything with you," was the basis of the negotiations, "with their help alone you will never get out of these constant scenes and conflicts. Perhaps you had better try the help of a stranger."

She accepted me forthwith as an ally against her parents, just as the little obsessional described above accepted me as an ally against her devil. The child's insight into her neurosis in the first case was replaced in the second by insight into conflict with the parents; but the active factor that both had in common was the amount of suffering, which in the first case stemmed from internal causes and in the second from external ones.

My procedure in the second case was essentially that recommended by Aichhorn (1925) for the treatment of delinquent children. He states that the worker entrusted with the care of such children must first of all take the side of the delinquent and assume that the child's attitude toward his environment is justified. Only in this way will he succeed in working *with* the child instead of *against* him.

I might emphasize here that in respect of this kind of work Aichhorn's position has considerable advantages over that of the analyst. He is authorized to intervene by the city and the state and his authority has official backing. In contrast, the analyst, as the child knows, is commissioned and paid by the parents; that means that he is in an awkward position if he takes a stand against his clients, even if this is ultimately in their own interest. In fact, whenever it was necessary to meet with the parents of this particular child, I felt uneasy; and finally after a few weeks, despite the child's own readiness for analysis, the treatment was abruptly terminated by the parents.

In any event, the necessary conditions for beginning a real analysis—the sense of suffering, confidence in analysis, and the decision to undertake it—were accomplished with little trouble in these two cases. I go now to the other extreme, i.e., a case in which none of these three factors was present.

This was a boy of 10 with an obscure mixture of many anxieties, nervous states, insincerities, and infantile perverse habits. Various small and one more serious theft had occurred in recent years. The conflict with his parents was neither open nor conscious, and on the surface any insight into his very uncomfortable condition, or any wish to change it, was not obvious. His attitude to me was thoroughly rejecting and mistrustful; all his strivings were directed toward protecting his sexual secrets from discovery.

Neither one of the two methods described above were applicable here. I could not ally myself with his conscious ego against a split-off part of his personality for he was not at all aware of any such division; nor could I offer myself as an ally against his surroundings, to which so far as he was consciously aware he was attached by the strongest feelings. I clearly had to take another course, more difficult and less direct, since what was needed was winning the boy's confidence by devious methods, and forcing myself upon a person who felt that he could do very well without me.

I tried this in various ways. At first, for a long time, I did nothing but follow his moods along all their paths and by-paths. If he came to his appointment in a cheerful mood, I was cheerful too; if he was serious or depressed, I acted seriously. If he preferred to spend the hour under the table, I would treat it as the most natural thing in the world, lift the tablecloth and speak to him under it. If he came with a string in his pocket, and began to show me remarkable knots and tricks, I would let him see that I could make more complicated knots and do more remarkable tricks. If he made faces, I pulled better ones; and if he challenged me to trials of strength, I showed myself incomparably stronger.

But I also followed his lead in every subject he talked about, from tales of pirates and questions of geography to stamp collections and love stories. In these conversations nothing was too grown-up or too delicate a subject for me to discuss, and not even his mistrustfulness could suspect an educational intention behind what I said. My attitude was like that of a film or novel meant to attract the audience or reader by catering to their baser interests. My first aim was in fact merely to make myself interesting to the boy. That in this initial period I also became familiar with many of his surface interests and inclinations was an unexpected but very welcome additional bonus.

After a time I introduced a second factor. I proved myself useful to him in small ways, wrote letters for him on the typewriter, was ready to help him with the writing down of daydreams and self-invented stories of which he was proud, and made all sorts of little things for him during his hour with me. In the case of a little girl who required a similar period of preparation I zealously crochetted and knitted during her appointments, and gradually clothed all her dolls and teddy bears.

To put it briefly, I developed a second quality agreeable to him: I was not only interesting, I had become useful. But in this second period I too had gained: by means of the letter and story writing I gradually obtained an introduction to his fantasy life.

Next came something even more important. I made him realize that being analyzed had great practical advantages; that, for example, punishable deeds have an altogther different and much more fortunate result when they are first told to the analyst, and only through him to those in charge of the child. Thus he became accustomed to relying on analysis as a protection from punishment and to claiming my help for repairing the consequences of his rash acts; he let me restore stolen money for him and got me to make all necessary but disagreeable confessions to his parents. At first, he repeatedly tested my abilities in this direction before he decided to believe in them.

After that, however, there were no more doubts; besides an interesting and useful companion I had become a very powerful person, without whose help he could no longer get along. Thus in these three capacities I had made myself indispensable to him and he had become dependent on me. But I had only waited for this moment to demand of him in return the most extensive cooperation, though not in words and not all at one stroke: I asked for the surrender, so necessary for analysis, of all his previously guarded secrets, which then took up the next weeks and months and with which the real analysis could finally begin.

You observe that in this case I was not at all concerned with establishing insight—in the course of our subsequent work this emerged of itself; here the aim was merely to create a tie strong enough to sustain the later analysis.

If this detailed description gives the impression that all the analyst is aiming at is the positive transference, I will try to erase this impression again with the help of other examples which hold a middle position between the two extremes mentioned.

I was called upon to analyze another boy of 10, who had recently developed a symptom which was unpleasant and disturbing to his environment: he had sudden noisy attacks of rage and defiance which broke out without any intelligible external reason and which in this otherwise inhibited and timid child were particularly striking. It was easy in this case to gain the child's confidence, since I was already known to him as his sister's analyst and since he was rather envious of the practical advantages which she clearly derived from the fact of being in treatment.

In spite of this I found no direct point of approach for the analysis, a fact for which the explanation was not hard to find. So far as his anxiety and his inhibitions were concerned, he had partial insight into them as well as some wish to get rid of them. But for his main symptom, the outbursts of rage, the opposite was true. He was unmistakably proud of these, regarded them as something which distinguished him from others (even if not precisely in a favorable sense), and enjoyed the worry they caused his parents. In this sense he felt the symptom to be "ego-syntonic" and at that time was ready to resist any attempt to rid him of it with analytic help.

Here too I adopted a somewhat devious and not very honest device to bring him into conflict with this part of his personality. I made him describe the outbreaks as often as they came and showed myself concerned and thoughtful. I inquired how far in such states he was in control of himself at all, and compared his fits of rage to those of a madman who would be beyond my aid. At that he was startled and rather frightened, for to be regarded as mad naturally did not accord with his ambitions. He began to try himself to master the outbreaks, to resist them instead of encouraging them as he had done before. As he did so, he realized his complete inability to suppress them and this failure enhanced his feelings of suffering and discomfort. After a few vain attempts the symptom finally, as I had intended, turned from a treasured possession into a disturbing foreign body, in the battle against which he only too readily claimed my help.

It will strike you that in this case a condition was induced by me which the obsessional girl had produced on her own: a split in the child's personality. In yet another case, that of a neurotic and difficult little girl of 7, I decided at the end of a long preparatory period to adopt a similar device. I suddenly separated off all her "badness" from herself, and personified it, under a name of its own. This was eventually successful insofar as she began to complain to me of this newly created person and obtained insight into the amount of suffering she endured on account of her. Once this insight was established, the child's analyzability was a natural consequence.

But let us not neglect another factor which may prove disturbing to the analysis, i.e., the child's loyalty conflicts. I encountered these in the treatment of a charming, highly sensitive little girl of 8 whose symptom was manifestly a tendency to have outbursts of crying on far too many occasions. She was eager for analytic help to combat this habit, but in spite of this, work with me did not proceed as expected. Whenever analysis attempted to probe into the depth, we came to an abrupt halt. I was already on the point of giving up when it emerged that the obstacle was her attachment to a rather conventional and strict nanny who resented the analysis. The child believed in our analytic discoveries and in me, but only up to the point at which the loyalty to the nanny came into question. Whatever went beyond aroused a tenacious and unassailable resistance. It was true that this repeated a loyalty conflict which had dominated her early childhood when she had had to choose between her parents after their separation. But this disclosure also did not wholly remove the obstacle since the nanny had become a very real and domineering figure in her life.

For the sake of the analysis, therefore, I entered into a deliberate battle with the aim of undermining the nanny's influence on the child. I awakened the girl's critical attitude, tried to shake her blind dependence, and turned to my account every one of the little conflicts which occur daily in a nursery. I knew that I had won, when one day the little girl told me again the story of such an encounter, but this time added, "Do you think she's right?" Only from then on could the analysis penetrate the depths, and finally lead to the most promising result of all the cases I have mentioned.

The decision whether such a battle for the child is a permissible method was in this case made without difficulty; the nanny's influence was undesirable not only for the analysis but for the whole development of the child. But consider how impossible such a situation becomes when the opponent is not a comparative stranger but one of the child's parents, or when one is faced with the question whether it is worth depriving the child, in the interests of a successful analysis, of an adult's otherwise favorable and desirable influence. We shall return to this question in more detail later.

I conclude the topic of this lecture with two more stories to show how far children are able to grasp the meaning of analysis and its therapeutic aim.

The first one comes from the case of the little obsessional patient. She recounted one day an unusually well-sustained battle with her devil, and suddenly demanded appreciation. "Anna Freud," she said, "am I not much stronger than my devil? Can't I control him very well by myself? I don't think I need you for it at all." I fully confirmed this. She was really much stronger than the devil now, even without me. "But I do need you," she said after pondering for a minute, "you have to help me not to be so unhappy about having to be stronger than he." I think that even an adult neurotic can show no better understanding of the change he expects from analysis.

The second story comes from the semidelinquent boy of 10, described above. One day in a later period of his analysis he entered into a conversation with one of my father's adult patients in the waiting room. This man told him about his dog, who had killed a fowl for which he, the owner, had had to pay. "The dog ought to be sent to

Freud," said my little patient, "he needs analysis." The adult patient did not reply, but afterward showed great disapproval. What odd sort of idea of analysis did the child have? The dog had nothing the matter with it; it wanted to kill the hen and it killed it. But I knew exactly what the boy had in mind. "The poor dog," he must have thought, "he wants so badly to be a good dog and he can't. Something inside him makes him kill chickens."

To his mind, insight into the inner conflict with forbidden wishes provided a fully sufficient motive for analysis.

The Methods of Child
Analysis

Ladies and Gentlemen: I imagine that my recent account will have left a very odd impression upon those among you who are practicing analysts. The procedures I presented to you contradict at too many points the rules of psychoanalytic technique as laid down for us in the past.

Let us review once more the various things I did:

I gave the little obsessional girl a positive promise of cure, based on the assumption that one cannot expect a child to follow a stranger on an unknown path to an uncertain end. At the same time I fulfilled her apparent desire to have authoritative demands imposed on her and thus to experience a sense of security. I openly offered myself as an ally, and joined the child in criticizing her parents.

In another case I embarked on a secret struggle with the home environment, and courted the child's affections in all possible ways.

In still another case, I exaggerated the severity of a symptom and frightened the patient, in order to accomplish my purposes.

And finally I insinuated myself into the children's trust and forced myself on people who were firmly convinced that they could do very well without me.

Where in all this is the delicate restraint prescribed for the analyst; the caution with which one holds out to the patient an uncertain prospect of the possibility of cure, or even of amelioration; the scrupulous discretion in all personal matters; the absolute frankness in evaluating the illness; and the full freedom which one gives the patient to break off the mutual work whenever he wishes to do so?

With regard to the latter, we do of course also maintain this with child patients, but it nevertheless remains more or less a fiction. The situation is somewhat like that in the school where one also wants children to believe that they are learning for themselves and their own lives and not for the benefit of the teachers and the school. If we took this too seriously, we would probably find the classroom empty next morning.

You may have come to suspect that I proceeded as I did either because I was ignorant of or unintentionally neglected the established rules. But I maintain that in order to suit a new situation I merely extended certain elements of an attitude that you all show to your patients, though without especially stressing it.

In my first lecture I may have exaggerated the difference between the child's initial situation and that of the adult. You know well that in the early days of an analysis the patient's determination and his trust appear to be quite fragile. We are in danger of losing him before he has begun the analysis at all, and we feel that we have gained a solid basis for our endeavor only when we have him firmly in a positive transference relationship. In these first days, however, we affect him, almost imperceptibly and without noticing that we are taking any special pains, in a number of ways which are not so very different from my laborious and apparently distinctive methods with children.

Take, for example, a severely depressed patient, though analytic therapy and technique are not directly designed for such cases. But if the treatment of such a case is undertaken, there may well be such a preparatory period in which the analyst by encouragement and sympathy with the patient's personal needs will attempt to arouse his interest in and decision for the analytic work.

Or take another case. As you know, our technical rules caution us against interpreting dreams too early and thereby offering the patient knowledge of his inner processes which he is not yet prepared to understand and therefore will reject. But with an intelligent and educated obsessional neurotic who doubts everything, we may be glad to be able to offer him, at the very outset of the treatment, an especially impressive dream interpretation. Thereby we interest him and satisfy his exacting intellectual demands—and basically we are doing nothing else but what the child analyst does when he shows a boy that he can do much cleverer tricks with a piece of string than the boy can himself.

Again, when we take the side of a rebellious and delinquent child and demonstrate our readiness to help him against his environment, we can find an analogous situation with adults. We show the adult neurotic too that we are there to help and support him; and we accept his version in all his conflicts with his family. In this case too, we make ourselves interesting and useful.

Even the matter of power and external authority plays a part. Observation shows that the experienced analyst with a reputation finds it much easier to hold his patient and to prevent his "absconding" in the early stages than the young beginner. Moreover, in the first hours the experienced analyst will be shown fewer "negative transference" manifestations and receive fewer expressions of hostility and mistrust than the beginner. We ascribe this difference to the young analyst's inexperience, his lack of tact in his demeanor toward the patient, his precipitous or overcautious interpretations. But I believe that here one should take the factor of external authority into account. The patient asks himself, not without reason, who this man is, after all, who suddenly claims to exercise such prodigious authority over him; and whether his claims are justified by his position in the world and the attitude of other, normal people toward him.

These doubts are not necessarily a matter of the re-emergence of old hostile impulses; they rather seem to me to be a manifestation of healthy critical common sense which asserts itself before the patient lets himself slide into the analytic transference situation. But the eminent analyst with a name and position obviously enjoys, by virtue of the esteem in which he is held, the same advantages as the child analyst, who in any case is bigger and older than his little patient, and who becomes a person of unquestioned power when the child feels that his authority is accepted by the parents even above their own.

These, then, would be the elements of a similar preparatory period in the treatment of adults. I believe, however, that I did not state the matter quite correctly. It would be more appropriate to say that in the technique of adult analysis we find *vestiges* of all the procedures which prove necessary with children. The extent to which we use them will depend upon the degree to which the adult patient with whom we are dealing is still an immature and dependent being and in this respect is closer to a child.

So much for the introductory phase to the treatment, i.e., the establishment of the analytic situation.

Let us now suppose that the child, by all the means described above, has really won confidence in the analyst, has acquired insight into his disturbance, and is now striving of his own accord for a change in his condition. So we come to our second theme—an examination of the means at our disposal for the analytic work proper with a child.

In the technique of adult analysis we have four such expedients. We turn to account whatever the patient's conscious memory can furnish for the establishment of as complete a history of his illness as possible; we employ dream interpretation; we assess and interpret the ideas brought up by the patient's free association; and, finally, through the interpretation of his transference reactions, we obtain access to all those parts of his past experience which can be translated into consciousness in no other way. I must inflict upon you in what follows a systematic examination of these expedients in their applicability to and utility for the analysis of children.

In the construction of the case history from the patient's conscious memories we come across the first difference. In adult cases, as you know, we refrain from obtaining any information at all from the patient's family and rely entirely upon what he can tell us himself. This voluntary restriction is based on the fact that communications imparted by the relatives are apt to be unreliable and incomplete and are colored by the relatives' personal attitude toward the patient.

But a child cannot contribute much to the history of his illness. His memory does not reach far back, until one comes to his aid with analysis. He is so taken up with the present that the past pales in comparison. Moreover, he himself does not know when his pathology began and when he first appeared to be different from other children. He is not yet inclined to compare himself with others, nor has he had much experience with self-imposed tasks by which he could measure his failures. The child analyst must in practice obtain the case history from the patient's parents. All he can do is to make allowances for possible inaccuracies and misrepresentations arising from personal motives.

When it comes to dream interpretation, on the other hand, we can apply unchanged to children what we have learned from our work with adults. During analysis the child dreams neither less nor more than the adult; and the transparency or obscurity of the dream content is, as in the case of adults, a reflection of the strength of the resistance. Children's dreams are certainly easier to interpret, though in analysis they are not always so simple as the examples given in *The Interpretation of Dreams*. We find in them all those distortions of wish fulfillment that correspond to the complicated neurotic organization of the child patient.

But there is nothing easier to make the child grasp than dream interpretation.

At the first account of a dream, I say, "No dream can make itself out of nothing; it must have fetched every bit from somewhere"—and then I set off with the child in search of its origins. The child amuses himself with the pursuit of the individual dream elements as with a jigsaw puzzle, and with great satisfaction follows up the separate images or words of the dream into real life situations.

Perhaps this comes about because the child still is nearer to dreams than the adult; it may again be merely because he feels no surprise to find a meaning in dreams, not having heard the view that they have no meaning. In any case he is proud of a successful dream interpretation. Incidentally, I have often found that even unintelligent children, who in all other respects were quite unsuited for analysis, did not fail in dream interpretation. I have conducted two such analyses for an extended period almost exclusively by using dreams.

But even where the child's associations to a dream fail to appear, an interpretation is nevertheless often possible. It is so much easier to know the child's situation, the daily happenings and significant people in his life. Often one may venture to insert the missing ideas into the interpretations from one's own knowledge of the situation. The following two examples of children's dreams merely serve to illustrate these circumstances.

In the fifth month of the analysis of a 9-year-old girl I eventually arrived at a discussion of her masturbation, which she could admit to herself only with a strong feeling of guilt. She felt very hot sensations when masturbating, and her revulsion against her handling of the genitals extended to these feelings. She began to be afraid of fire and rebelled against wearing warm clothes. She could not look at the flame burning in a gas water heater next to her bedroom without fearing an explosion. One evening when the mother was away the nanny wanted to light the heater, but did not know how and called the elder brother to help. But he did not know how either. The little girl stood by and had the feeling that she ought to know how to do it.

The following night she dreamed of this same situation, but in the dream she actually did help; but did it wrong and the heater exploded. As a punishment the nanny held her in the fire to make her burn up. She woke up in a state of great anxiety and awakened her mother at once to tell her the dream, adding (from her analytic knowledge) that it was certainly a punishment dream. She brought up no other ideas, but I could easily supply them in this case.

Manipulating the heater stood for manipulating her own body, which she assumed her brother did too. "Doing it wrong" was the expression of her own condemnation, and the explosion probably represented her form of orgasm. The nurse, who had admonished against masturbation, appropriately carried out the punishment.

Two months later she had another fire dream with the following content:

On the radiator there were two bricks of different colors. I knew that the house was going to catch fire and I was frightened. Then somebody came and took the bricks away.

When she woke up, she had her hand on her genitals.

This time she associated to a part of the dream, the bricks; she had been told that if you put bricks on your head, you do not grow. From that the interpretation could be completed without difficulty. To stop growing was one of the punishments for masturbation which she feared, and we recognized the significance of fire as a symbol of her sexual excitation from the earlier dream. Thus she masturbated in her sleep, was warned by the remembrance of all the prohibitions, and was frightened. The unknown person who took away the bricks was probably myself, with my soothing reassurances.

Not all dreams occurring in the analysis of children present so few difficulties in interpretation. But on the whole my little obsessional was right when she would announce to me a dream of the preceding night as follows: "Today I have had a funny dream, but you and I will soon find out what it all means."

The interpretation of daydreams as well as of ordinary dreams plays an important part in the analysis of children. Several of the children with whom I gained my experience were great daydreamers, and the account of their fantasies was of the greatest assistance to me in their analyses. It is usually very easy to induce children to recount their daydreams, once one has gained their confidence in other matters. They tell them more readily and are clearly less ashamed of them than adults, who condemn daydreaming as "childish." While the adult, because of this condemnation, usually brings his daydreams into the analysis only at a late stage and hesitatingly, in a child's analysis their appearance is often of great assistance in the difficult early stages. The following examples illustrate three types of such fantasies.

The simplest type is the daydream as a reaction to the day's experience. The little girl, for example, whose fire dreams are mentioned above, reacted with the following daydream at a time when competition with her brothers and sisters was playing a very important role in her analysis:

> I wish I had never come into the world at all, I wish I could die. Sometimes I pretend I do die, and then come back into the world as an animal or a doll. But if I come back into the world as a doll, I know who I mean to belong to—a little girl with whom my nurse was before, who is specially nice and good. I want to be her doll and I would not mind at all being treated like they treat dolls. I would be a dear little baby and they could wash me and do anything to me. The little girl would like me best of all. Perhaps she would get another doll for Christmas, but I would still be her favorite. She would never prefer any doll to the baby doll.

Her current situation could not find clearer expression in any account or association than it did in this little fantasy.

The 6-year-old obsessional patient lived at the beginning of her analysis with friends of her family. She had one of her fits of naughtiness, which was much criticized by the other children. Her little girlfriend even refused to sleep in the same room with her, which upset her very much. In the analysis, however, she told me that because she had been so good, the nanny had given her a present of a little toy rabbit; at the same time she assured me that the other children liked sleeping with her very much. Then she recounted a daydream which she had suddenly had while she was resting. She did not even know that she was making it up.

> Once upon a time there was a little rabbit, whose family was not at all nice to him. They were going to send him to the butcher and have him slaughtered. But he found it out. He had a car which was very old, but it could still be driven. He went for it at night and got in and drove

away. He came to a dear little house in which a little girl [here she used her own name] lived. She heard him crying downstairs and came down and let him in. Then he stayed to live with her.

Here the feeling of being unwanted, which she would willingly be spared both in my eyes and her own, shows itself quite transparently. She herself is twice present in the daydream—as the little unloved rabbit and as the little girl who treats him as well as she herself would like to be treated.

A more complicated second type is the continued daydream. With children who compose such "serial story" daydreams it is often very easy to get on such terms that even in the earliest part of the analysis they will daily recount a new installment. These day-by-day continuations can then be used to reconstruct the current inner situation of the child.[1]

As an example of a third type I will mention a 9-year-old boy, whose daydreams were concerned with very different people and circumstances but which nevertheless reached the same outcome in many different situations. He began his analysis with the narration of an abundance of such stored-up fantasies. In many of them the two principal personages were a hero and a king. The king threatened the hero, wanting to torture and slay him, and the hero escaped him in all possible ways. All new technical inventions, especially an air fleet, played an important part in the pursuit, as did a cutting machine which when in motion sent out sicklelike knives on each side. The fantasy ended with the hero victorious, and doing everything to the king which the king wanted to do to him.

[1] For a detailed example, see ch. 1 in Part III of this volume.

Another of his daydreams depicted a teacher who punished and beat the children. The children eventually surrounded and overpowered her, and beat her to death.

Still another had to do with a whipping machine, in which in the end the torturer was locked instead of the captive for whom it was intended. He still possessed in his memory a whole collection of such fantasies with endless variations.

Without knowing anything more about the boy we can divine that all these fantasies are based on the defense against and revenge for a castration threat; that is to say, the castration is to be carried out in the daydream on the very person who originally threatened it. You will agree that with such a beginning one can anticipate much of the subsequent course of the analysis.

A further technical aid, which besides the use of dreams and daydreams comes very much to the fore in many of my analyses of children, is drawing; in three of my cases this almost took the place of all other communications for some time.

Thus the little fire dreamer, at the time when she was occupied with her castration complex, incessantly drew pictures of a fearful-looking monster in human shape, with protruding chin, long nose, piles of hair, and a frightful set of teeth. The name of this constantly recurring monster was "Bitey," and his function was clearly to bite off the male genital which in manifold fashion appeared all over his own body.

Another series of drawings which she made in great quantity during her visits, either as an accompaniment to her stories or in silence, portrayed all sorts of beings, children, birds, snakes, and dolls, all with enormously elongated arms and legs or beaks and tails.

During the same period she once suddenly drew on a page all the things she wanted to be: a boy (so as to possess a male member), a doll (so as to be the best-beloved), a dog (which to her represented virility), and a sailor boy, whom she took from a fantasy in which as a boy she alone accompanied her father on a voyage around the world. Above all these figures was yet another drawing from a half-heard and half-invented fairy story—a witch who was pulling out a giant's hair; thus again a representation of castration for which at that time she blamed her mother. In strange contrast to this was a series of pictures from a much later period, in which a queen presented to a little princess standing before her a marvelous long-stemmed flower (obviously another penis-symbol).

The little obsessional neurotic drew pictures of another kind. She occasionally accompanied her anal fantasies, which took up the first part of her analysis, with illustrations. For example, she portrayed an anal land of Cockaigne, in which instead of the mounds of porridge and tarts of the fairy story the people had to eat their way through a monstrous accumulation of pats of excrement arranged in rows. In addition to these drawings, however, she made a series of most delicately colored pictures of flowers and gardens, which she painstakingly executed with much neatness and animation while detailing to me her very "dirty" anal daydreams.

But I fear that I have sketched for you, thus far, too ideal a picture of the conditions obtaining in the analysis of children. In this picture the family readily provides all requisite information; the child is disclosed as an eager dream interpreter bringing a rich outpouring of daydreams and furnishing a series of interesting drawings, from all of which conclusions about his unconscious impulses can be drawn. If all this is so, it is puzzling why child analysis should always have been regarded as an especially difficult area, or why so many analysts declare that they can make no headway in the treatment of children.

The solution is not far to seek. The child cancels all the foregoing advantages by reason of the fact that he refuses to do free association. He perplexes the analyst by virtue of the fact that the very method on which the analytic technique is founded can to all intents and purposes not be applied. It is obviously contrary to a child's nature to assume the comfortable recumbent position prescribed for the adult, to expunge by an effort of his own will all criticism of the emerging ideas, to exclude nothing from his communications, and so to explore the surface of his consciousness.

It is indeed true that when one has attached a child to oneself in the ways I have described, and made oneself indispensable to him, one can make him do almost anything. Thus he will occasionally associate on being invited to do so, for a short time and to please the analyst. Such an interpolation of associations can certainly be very useful and lead to sudden enlightenment in a difficult situation. But such assistance will be an isolated, temporary occurrence; it will never be the secure foundation on which the whole analytic work can be based.

I had a little girl in analysis who proved to be particularly docile and amenable to my wishes. She was a very talented drawer and visually especially perceptive. Occasionally I would ask her to "see pictures." She would then close her eyes and sit herself down in an odd crouching position and follow attentively her inner images. In this way she once actually gave me the solution to a long-drawn-out period of resistance. This was the phase of treatment occupied with the struggle over masturbation and the detachment from her nanny, to whom she had retreated once more with redoubled affection so as to defend herself against my efforts at liberation. I asked her to see pictures and the first one that emerged elicited the answer: "Nanny is flying away over the sea." This, augmented by a vision of myself surrounded by a lot of dancing devils, meant that I would be sending the nurse away; and then she would have no defense against her temptation to masturbate and would be made "wicked" by me.

Here and there, and more frequently than these deliberate and invited associations, others, unintentional and uninvited, come to our help. I again take the little obsessional neurotic as an example. At the climax of her analysis it became essential to confront her with her hatred of her mother, against the knowledge of which she had previously protected herself by the creation of her "devil," the impersonal representative of all her hostile impulses. Although until then she had cooperated readily, at this point she became quite reluctant and resistive. At the same time, however, she relapsed at home into all manner of defiant behavior, from which I daily proved to her that one could only hate a person whom one treated so badly. Finally, confronted with these constantly recurring proofs, she gave way, but now she wanted me to tell her why she would have such hostile feelings for her mother whom she professed to love very much. Here I declined to give further information, for I too was at the end of my knowledge. Thereupon after a moment's silence she said, "You know, I believe it is the fault of a dream I once had [some weeks earlier] that we never understood." I asked her to repeat it, which she did:

All my dolls were there and my rabbit as well. Then I went away and the rabbit began to cry most dreadfully;

and I was so sorry for it. [She now added:] I believe I am always copying the rabbit now, and that is why I keep crying like it did.

In reality of course it was the other way round—the rabbit copied her, not she the rabbit. In that dream she herself had taken the mother's place, and treated the rabbit as she had been treated by her mother. With this dream idea she had finally found the reproach which her consciousness always shrank from making against her mother: that she had always gone away just when the child needed her most.

Some days later she repeated the process a second time. When after a momentary sense of liberation her mood became quite gloomy again, I urged her to try to contribute more on the same subject. She could not do so, but said suddenly in deep thought, "It is so lovely at G., I should like so much to go there again." On closer questioning it became apparent that during a holiday in that place she must have passed one of her unhappiest times. Her elder brother who had had whooping cough had been sent back to town to his parents, and she was isolated with a nanny and two younger siblings. She added spontaneously, "The nanny was always cross when I took the toys away from the little ones." Thus at that time the nanny's actual preference for the younger children was added to the parents' supposed preference for the brother. She felt herself neglected on all sides and reacted in her own way. Once again she had found one of her deepest reproaches against her mother through a recollection, this time of the beauty of the countryside in G.

I would not emphasize these three instances of surprising associations if similar instances occurred more frequently in the analysis of children. In analyzing adults they are, of course, the rule.

This absence of the child's readiness for free association has led everyone concerned with the problem of child analysis to seek for some substitute or other. Hermine Hug-Hellmuth attempted to replace the knowledge obtained from an adult patient's free associations by playing with the child, seeing him in his own home, and trying to become familiar with all his intimate daily circumstances. Melanie Klein substitutes for the adult association technique the play technique with children described in her publications. She starts from the premise that action is more natural for a little child than speech, and puts at his disposal a host of tiny playthings, a world in miniature, thereby creating for him the opportunity to act in this play world. Equating all the actions which the child carries out in this way with the adult's spoken ideas, she accompanies them with interpretations as we are used to do with adult patients. It looks at first sight as though a distressing gap in the technique of child analysis had been filled in an unobjectionable way. I wish to reserve, however, for my next lecture an examination of the theoretical foundation of this play technique, and to set it in relation to the last aspect of our present subject, the role of transference in the analysis of children.

The Role of Transference in
the Analysis of Children

Ladies and Gentlemen: I shall briefly go over the ground covered at our last meeting.

Focusing on the methods of child analysis, we learned that the child analyst is forced to piece together the history of the child's illness from information furnished by the parents instead of relying exclusively on information given by the patient; we became familiar with the child as a good dream interpreter, and evaluated the significance of daydreams and imaginative drawings as technical aids. On the other hand, I had to report that children are not inclined to enter into free association, and by this refusal force us to look for some substitute for this most essential of aids in the analysis of adults. We concluded with a description of one of these substitute methods, postponing its theoretical evaluation until today.

The play technique worked out by Melanie Klein is undoubtedly very valuable for observing the child. Instead of taking the time and trouble to pursue him into his home environment, we establish at one stroke the whole of his known world in the analyst's room, and let him move about in it under the analyst's eye—at first without any intervention. In this way we have the opportunity of getting to know the child's various reactions, the strength of his aggressive impulses or of his affections, as well as his attitude to the various objects and persons represented by the toys. To observe the child thus at play also has other advantages over watching him in his home background. The toys are easily manipulated by the child and subject to his will, so that he can carry out with them all the actions which in the real world are banned and remain confined to fantasy. All these merits make the use of the Kleinian play technique virtually indispensable to us for familiarizing ourselves with small children, for whom action is more natural than verbal expression.

Melanie Klein, however, goes one step further in the employment of this technique. She assumes that these play actions of the child are equivalent to the free associations of the adult patient, and persists in translating every action that the child performs into the corresponding thoughts; that is to say, she attempts to find the symbolic content underlying each single move in the play. If the child overturns a lamppost or a toy figure, she interprets this action, e.g., as an aggressive impulse against the father; a deliberate collision between two cars as evidence of the child having observed sexual intercourse between the parents. Her procedure consists of accompanying the child's activities with translations and interpretations, which—like the interpretations of the adult's free association—exert a directing influence on the further course of the patient's inner processes.

Let us examine the justification for equating the child's play activity with the adult's free association. The adult's ideas are "free"; that is to say, the patient has switched off all conscious control and influence over his thoughts, but at the same time he nevertheless has a certain goal in mind: his associations are influenced by his being in analysis. But the child does not have a goal in mind. At the beginning of these lectures I have explained how I attempt to give the child patient some idea of the purpose and aim of analysis. But the young children for whom Melanie Klein has worked out her play technique are still too immature to be influenced in this way. M. Klein considers it as one of the important advantages of her method that she does not need such a preparation of the child.

On the other hand, if the child's play is not dominated by the same purposive attitude as the adult's free association, there is no justification for treating it as having the same significance. Instead of being invariably invested with symbolic meaning, it may sometimes admit of harmless explanations. The child who upsets a toy lamppost may have witnessed some such incident in the street the day before; the car collision may be reproducing a similar happening; the child who opens the handbag of a lady visitor is not necessarily, as M. Klein maintains, expressing his curiosity whether his mother's womb conceals another baby; he may be repeating an experience of the previous day when a similar visitor brought him a present in a similar receptacle. Indeed, with adults too we do not feel justified in ascribing symbolic significance to every one of their acts or ideas, but do so only to those that arise under the influence of the analytic situation which he has accepted.

I realize that these objections to the Kleinian play technique could be met by counterarguments. One could argue that even if the child's play is open to the harmless interpretations suggested, the fact remains that he reproduces just those particular scenes in his analytic session. Is it not precisely the symbolic significance of the experiences which causes them to be preferred over others and to be reenacted? It is true, the argument might continue, that the child's actions lack the purposive goal of the analytic situation, which guides the adult. But perhaps he does not need it at all. The adult has to make a conscious effort not to control his thoughts and leave them entirely to be directed by his unconscious impulses. But the child may require no such deliberate modification of the situation since he may at all times and in all of his activities be under the domination of unconscious strivings.

As you see, an exchange of theoretical arguments does not easily settle the question whether it is justified to equate the child's play actions with the adult's free associations. This issue obviously must be left to be reviewed in the light of practical experience.

A critique might start at another point. We know that in addition to all the activities which the child carries out with the toys, Melanie Klein also uses as material for interpretation whatever the child does in relation to the objects in the treatment room and to her own person. Here again she follows strictly the example of adult analysis. We cer-

tainly feel justified in drawing into the analysis all the behavior and attitudes the patient shows toward us, including
all the small voluntary or involuntary actions which we see
him perform. In doing this, we rely on the state of transference in which he finds himself, a condition which can
invest even otherwise trivial behavior with symbolic significance.

At this point, however, we must ask whether a child
finds himself in the same transference situation as the adult;
in what manner and forms his transference manifestations
are expressed; and in what way they lend themselves to interpretation. It is these questions which open up our most
important topic—the role of transference as a technical aid
in the analysis of children. Whether we support or oppose
Melanie Klein's views will, to a large extent, depend on the
stand we take with regard to it.

You remember from my first lecture that I take great
pains to establish in the child a strong attachment to myself, and to bring him into a relationship of dependence
on me. I would not try so hard to do this, if I thought the
analysis of children could be carried out outside a relationship of this kind. This affectionate attachment, i.e., the
positive transference to the analyst, becomes the prerequi-
site for all later analytic work. Children, in fact, believe
only the people they love, and make efforts only for the
love of such people.

The analysis of children needs much more of this positive element than is the case with adults. Side by side with
the analytic work, we also pursue a goal which might be
called reeducational (to be dealt with later in greater detail). The success of upbringing always—not only in child

analysis—stands or falls with the child's attachment to the person in charge of him. And with regard to child analysis, we cannot say that for our purposes it is enough merely to establish a transference, regardless of whether it is friendly or hostile. We know that with an adult we can work for prolonged periods of time with a negative transference, which we turn to our account through consistent interpretation and reference to its origins. But with a child negative impulses toward the analyst—however revealing they may be in many respects—are essentially disturbing and should be dealt with analytically as soon as possible. The really fruitful work always takes place in positive attachment.

In connection with the preparatory period I have already described how we establish this tie. Its manifestation in fantasies and small or larger actions is hardly distinguishable from the equivalent processes in adult patients. The negative manifestations are encountered whenever we attempt to assist a fragment of repressed material toward liberation from the unconscious, thereby drawing upon ourselves the resistance of the ego. At such a time we appear to the child as the dangerous and feared tempter, and we receive all the expressions of hatred and repulsion with which at other times he regards his own forbidden instinctual impulses.

In what follows I present a detailed example of a positive transference fantasy from the 6-year-old obsessional girl mentioned several times. The external occasion for this fantasy was furnished by myself, for I had visited her in her own home and stayed for her evening bath. She opened her hour on the next day with the words, "You visited me in my bath and next time I'll come and visit you in yours."

A little later she told me a daydream which she had composed in bed before going to sleep, after I had left. I add her own explanatory asides in brackets.

All the rich people did not like you. And your father who was very rich did not like you at all. [That means I am angry with your father, don't you think?] And you liked no one and gave lessons to no one. And my parents hated me and so did John and Billy and Mary and all the people in the world hated us, even the people who did not know us, even dead people. So you liked only me and I liked only you and we always stayed together. All the others were very rich, but we two were quite poor. We had nothing, not even clothes because they took away everything we had. There was only the couch left in the room and we slept on that together. But we were very happy together. And then we thought we ought to have a baby. So we mixed a big job and a little job to make a baby. But then we thought that was not a nice thing to make a baby out of. So we began to mix flower petals and other things and that gave me a baby. For the baby was in me. It stayed in me quite a long while [my mother told me that babies stay quite a long while in their mothers]; and then the doctor came and took it out. But I was not a bit sick [mothers usually are, my mother said]. The baby was very sweet and cute and so we thought we'd like to be just as cute and changed ourselves to be very tiny. I was "so" high and you were "so" high. [I think that is because we found out that I want to be as small as Billy and Mary.] And since we had nothing at all, we started to make ourselves a house out of roseleaves, and beds out of roseleaves and pillows and mattresses all out of roseleaves sewn together. Where the little holes were left we put something white in. Instead of wallpaper we had the thinnest glass and the walls were carved in different patterns. The chairs too were made of glass, but we were so light that we were not too heavy for them. [I think my mother does not appear at all because I was angry with her yesterday.]

Then there followed a detailed description of the furniture and all the other things that were made for the house. The daydream was obviously spun out in this direction until she went to sleep, laying special emphasis on the point that our initial poverty was finally made up for and that in the end we had much nicer things than all the rich people she had mentioned at the beginning.

At other times, however, the same little patient related how she was warned against me from within. The inner voice said, "Don't believe Anna Freud. She tells lies. She will not help you and will only make you worse. She will change your face too, so that you look uglier. Everything she says is not true. Just be tired, stay quietly in bed, and don't go to her today." But she always told this voice to be silent and said to it that it should wait for the next session to tell me all these things.

At a time when another child patient and I were discussing masturbation, I appeared in the girl's imagination in all sorts of degrading roles—as a beggar, as a poor old woman, and once as just myself but standing in the middle of my room with devils dancing around me.

Thus we become, as in the analysis of adults, the target of the patient's friendly or hostile impulses, depending upon his inner circumstances. On the basis of these examples we would say that a child makes a good transference. Unfortunately, that is not really true. The child does enter into the liveliest relations with the analyst; he expresses a multitude of reactions which he has acquired in the relationship with his parents; he gives us most important hints on the formation of his character in the fluctuation, intensity, and expression of his feelings; but he forms no transference neurosis.

The analysts among you will know what I mean by this. The adult neurotic gradually transforms, in the course of analytic treatment, the symptoms on account of which he sought this remedy. He gives up the old objects on which his fantasies were hitherto fixed, and centers his neurosis anew upon the person of the analyst. As we put it, he replaces his previous symptoms with tranference symptoms, transposes his existing neurosis, of whatever kind, into a transference neurosis, and displays all his abnormal reactions in relation to the new transference person, the analyst. On this new ground, where the analyst feels at home, he can together with the patient trace the development and growth of the individual symptoms; and on this cleared field of operations then takes place the final struggle for gradual insight into the unconscious pathogenic processes.

We can cite two theoretical reasons why the same course of events does not automatically occur in the small child. One lies within the psychological structure of the child himself; the other, in the child analyst's behavior.

Unlike the adult, the child is not ready to produce a new edition of his love relationships, because, as one might say, the old edition is not yet exhausted. His original objects, the parents, are still real and present as love objects—not only in fantasy as with the adult neurotic; between them and the child exist all the relations of everyday life, and all the gratifications and disappointments in reality still depend on them. The analyst enters this situation as a new person, and will probably share with the parents the child's love or hate. But there is no necessity for the child to put the analyst fully in the parents' place, since compared to them he has not the same advantages which the adult finds when he can exchange his fantasy objects for a real person.

Let us in this connection reconsider M. Klein's method. She believes that when a child shows hostility toward her in the first hour, repulsing or even beginning to strike her, one may see in that proof of the child's ambivalent attitude toward his mother, the hostile component of this being displaced onto the analyst. But I believe the truth of the matter is different. The more tenderly a little child is attached to his own mother, the fewer friendly impulses he has toward strangers. We see this most clearly with the baby, who shows only anxious rejection toward everyone other than his mother or nurse. Indeed, the converse obtains. It is especially with children who are accustomed to little loving treatment at home, and are not used to showing or receiving any strong affection, that a positive relationship is often most quickly established. They obtain from the analyst what they have until now expected in vain from the original objects.

There are other reasons why transference to the child analyst does not readily lend itself to interpretation. We know how we behave in the analysis of adults for this purpose. We remain impersonal and shadowy, a blank page on which the patient can inscribe his transference fantasies, somewhat in the way in which a motion picture is projected upon an empty screen. We avoid issuing prohibitions and allowing gratifications. If in spite of this we seem to the patient forbidding or encouraging, it is then easy to make it clear to him that he has brought the material for this impression from his own past.

But the child analyst must be anything but a shadow. We have already heard that for the child he is an interesting person, endowed with all sorts of impressive and attractive qualities. The educational implications which, as you will hear, are involved in the analysis, result in the child knowing very well just what seems desirable or undesirable to the analyst, and what he sanctions or disapproves of. And such a well-defined and in many respects novel person is unfortunately a poor transference object, that is, of little use when it comes to interpreting the transference. The difficulty here is, as though, to use our former illustration, the screen on which a film was to be projected already bore another picture. The more elaborate and brightly colored it is, the more will it tend to efface the outlines of what is superimposed.

For these reasons the child forms no transference neurosis. In spite of all his positive and negative impulses toward the analyst, he continues to display his abnormal reactions where they were displayed before—in the home. Because of this the child analyst must not only take into account what happens under his own eye but also direct his attention to the area where the neurotic reactions are to be found—the child's family. Here we have come upon the source of the innumerable technical difficulties in the analysis of children, practical problems which I can describe only in broad outlines.

If we accept this point of view—that the child is still dependent on his real objects—then we are dependent on a permanent news service about the child; we must know the people in his environment and have some idea of their reactions to the child. In the ideal case, we share our work with the persons who are actually bringing up the child; just as we share with them the child's affection or hostility.

Where the external conditions or the personalities of the

parents do not allow such cooperation, certain material for the analysis eludes us. On this account I had to conduct some analyses of children almost exclusively by means of dreams and daydreams. There was nothing interpretable in the transference and much of the day-to-day symptomatic neurotic material never became available to me.

But there are ways and means of bringing about in the child a situation which approximates the more favorable one of adult analysis with its transference neurosis. This may come into play when we are dealing with a severe neurotic illness in a child whose environment is hostile either to analysis or to the child. In such an instance, the child may have to be removed from his family and be placed in a suitable institution. As there is no such institution in existence at present, we are at full liberty to imagine one, say a home supervised by the child analyst himself, or—less far-fetched—a school which is organized according to psychoanalytic principles and geared to cooperation with the analyst. In both cases we would first see a symptom-free period, in which the child adapts himself to the new and favorable surroundings. The better he feels at this time, the more unsuitable and unwilling for analysis shall we find him. We shall probably do best to leave him quite undisturbed until he has "acclimatized himself," and until under the influence of the realities of everyday life he has formed an attachment to the new environment, beside which the original objects gradually pale. He will then allow his symptoms to revive again and center his abnormal reactions on the new persons; in other words, he will develop a new edition of his neurosis which is open to analysis.

In an institution of the first sort, directed by the child analyst—desirable or wholly undesirable as this may be—

the reenactment of the pathology would be a genuine transference neurosis in the sense in which we use this term in
relation to adults—with the analyst as focal object. In the
other case we should simply have artificially bettered the
home environment, by creating a substitute home which al-
lows us to see into it, as far as this seems necessary for the
analytic work, with substitute parents whose reactions toward the child we could influence.

Thus the removal of a disturbed child from his home
might appear to be the most practical solution.

But when we come to consider the termination of a child's
analysis, we shall see how many objections there are to it.
By this expedient we would precipitate the child's natural
development at a crucial stage—we would force the child
to detach himself prematurely from the parental objects at
a time when he neither is capable of any independence in
his emotional life, nor has at his disposal any freedom in
the choice of new love objects. Even if we insisted on a
very long duration for the analysis of children, in most cases
there would still remain a hiatus between its termination
and the beginning of adulthood, a period during which the
child needs education, protection, and guidance in every
sense of the words.

There is no assurance that after we have secured a successful resolution of the transference, the child will find his
own way to the right objects. He returns home at a time
when he has become a stranger there; and his further guidance may be entrusted to the very persons from whom we
have forcibly detached him. On inner grounds he is not
capable of self-reliance. We would thus be placing him in
a position of renewed difficulty, in which he would again

find most of the conditions that originally gave rise to his conflicts. So he could once more take either the path to neurosis, or, if this is closed to him by the successful outcome of the analytic treatment, the opposite line of open rebellion. From the purely therapeutic point of view, this may seem an improvement; but from the aspect of social adjustment which after all is demanded from every child, it will not appear in that light.

4

Child Analysis and the
Upbringing of Children

Ladies and Gentlemen: We have so far, considered two aspects of the analysis of children and today I will turn to the third and perhaps most important.

Let me once more retrace our progress. The first part was concerned, as you may remember, with the introductory phase in the analysis of children, the activities during that period being wholly "unanalytic." I described actions and occupations, such as crochetting, knitting, games, as well as the various means of enticement, not because I consider them important for analysis, but rather to show what a difficult subject the child is, how he refuses to respond even to the best methods of scientific therapy, and absolutely requires that his own childish peculiarities be appropriately matched. Whatever we embark on with a child, whether we teach him arithmetic or geography, whether we intend to educate or analyze, we must always first establish a very definite emotional relationship with him. The harder the work, the greater will be the strain exerted on this attachment. The introduction to the treatment, i.e., the establishment of this tie, thus follows its own rules, which are determined by the child's nature and at this point not yet by psychoanalytic theory and technique.

The second part of my exposition dealt with analysis proper, and surveyed the paths whereby a child's unconscious can be approached. It was disappointing for you to learn, I noticed, that the most important and significant techniques for the analysis of adults are not available for that of children, that we fall short of many scientific requirements and obtain our material where we can find it— much as we do in ordinary life if we wish to acquire detailed knowledge of another person.

I suspect that this disappointment also refers to another matter. Since I have practiced child analysis, I have often been asked by analytic colleagues whether this work does not yield more knowledge than can be gained from adults of the developmental processes of the first two years of life, which increasingly have become the object of our analytic investigations. The child, they say, is still much nearer to this significant period, his repressions still far less deeply embedded, the access to the material superimposed on these earlier layers must be so much easier, and child analysis must surely offer untold opportunities for gaining new information.

So far I have always had to answer these questions with

a negative. The material which the child brings us is indeed, as you may have noticed from my illustrations, especially clear and unequivocal and throws a good deal of light on the content of the infantile neuroses. He brings much welcome confirmation of facts, which until now we have been able to assert only on the basis of reconstructions from the analysis of adults. But so far as my experience goes, and with the technique I have described, it does not take us beyond the boundaries where verbalization begins—that period, in other words, when his thought processes begin to approximate our own.

This limitation is not difficult to explain theoretically. What we learn in the analysis of adults about this "prehistoric" period is brought to light through free associations and the interpretation of the transference reactions—that is to say, through the aid of precisely those two means which leave us in the lurch in the analysis of children. Besides, our situation may in this respect be compared to that of an ethnologist, who would also seek in vain for a short-cut to an understanding of prehistory by studying a primitive people instead of a highly civilized culture. When studying the primitives he will feel the absence of the elaborate body of myths and sagas which in the case of civilized people usually help in drawing conclusions about their prehistory.

Similarly with the small child, we lack the reaction formations and cover memories which are constructed only in the course of the latency period, and from which the later analysis can extract the material condensed in them. Here again, therefore, the analysis of children offers no advantage over that of adults, but is in fact less able to extract unconscious material.

And now for the third aspect, the utilization of the analytic material which we have brought to light by means of such cumbersome preparation and by so many paths and bypaths. You will by now be prepared to hear a good deal that is unexpected and deviates from the classical rules.

Let us first reconsider in rather more detail the corresponding situation in the adult patient. His neurosis is, as we know, entirely an internal affair. It is played out between three factors, his instinctual unconscious, his ego, and the superego, which represents the ethical and aesthetic demands of society. The task of analysis is to raise the conflict between these protagonists to a higher level, by making conscious what is unconscious. The instinctual impulses were until now repressed and therefore removed from the influence of the superego. Analysis frees them and makes them accessible to the influence of the superego which henceforth will determine their further fate. Repression is replaced by conscious critique, which will reject some of the instinctual impulses, sublimate others, and having divested a part of them of their sexual aims allow them gratification. This favorable outcome is to be ascribed to the fact of ego maturation. Between the time when the repressions were originally instituted and the time when analysis achieves liberation, ego and superego have undergone their whole ethical and intellectual development, and so are in a position to make other decisions than those which were originally open to them. The instinctual wishes will submit to various modifications, and the superego surrender many of its exaggerated demands. Thus, on the common ground of consciousness a synthesis between the two is brought about.

And now compare this condition with that of the child

patient. The child's neurosis also is an internal affair, determined by the same three forces, the instinctual life, the ego, and the superego. But at two points we have already been prepared to find that in the child's case the outer world penetrates deeply into his inner situation and becomes an integral part of it, as inconvenient as this may be for the analysis. In discussing the introductory phase we had to ascribe so important a factor as insight into the illness, not to the child himself, but to the people around him; and in describing the transference situation we demonstrated that the analyst must share the child's available hostile and loving impulses with the original objects of these feelings. We are thus not surprised to learn that the outer world affects the mechanism of the infantile neurosis and the analysis more deeply than is the case in adults.

We have said that the superego of an adult individual has become the representative of the moral demands made by the society in which he lives. We know that it owes its origin to the identification with the first and most important love objects of the child, the parents; to them society has transferred the task of establishing its current ethical claims and enforcing restrictions upon the drives. Thus what was originally a personal obligation felt toward the parents becomes, in the course of development, an ego ideal that is independent of its prototypes in the external world.

In the case of a child, however, there is as yet no such independence. Detachment from the first love objects still lies in the future, and identification with them is accomplished only gradually and piecemeal. Even though the superego already exists and interacts with the ego at this early period much as it does in later times, its dependence on the objects to which it owes its existence must not be over-looked: we might compare it to that between two con-nected receptacles. If externally the level of good relations with the parents rises, so does the internal status of the superego and the energy with which it enforces its claims. If the former is lowered, the superego is diminished as well.

Let us take the infant as the first example. When the mother or nurse has succeeded in accustoming the little child to the control of his excretory functions, we soon get the impression that he fulfills these requirements of clean-liness not only for the sake of the adult (for love or fear of her), but that he himself takes some interest in the matter, is pleased with his own cleanliness or vexed if he has an "accident." We can observe over and over again, however, that a subsequent separation from the person who has initi-ated sphincter control, such as a temporary removal from the mother or a change of nurse, puts the new achievement in jeopardy. The child will become just as dirty as he was before he was toilet trained and will relearn what he had previously mastered only when the mother returns or when he has formed an attachment to the new nurse. Neverthe-less, the impression that the child demanded cleanliness of himself was not altogether deceptive. The inner prompting exists, but it is valued by the child only as long as the per-son responsible for the establishment of the demands is actually present in reality. When he loses the relationship to this object, he also loses his pleasure in fulfilling the obligation.

But even as late as at the beginning of the latency period the same conditions prevail. The analysis of adults provides ample confirmation of the fact that a disturbance in the child's ties to his parents critically affects moral development and character formation. If at this time he loses his parents through separation of any kind, or if as objects they are depreciated in his eyes, perhaps through mental illness or criminality, his partly erected superego is in danger of being lost or depreciated too; as a result the child lacks a firm internal structure to control the instinctual impulses which press for satisfaction. This may provide an explanation for the origin of some dissocial tendencies and character deformations.

To illustrate such conditions which may exist even at the end of the latency period, I use an example given by Aichhorn (1925) from his dealings with a preadolescent boy. Aichhorn asked the boy whether he was ever aware of any thoughts which one would prefer not to have. The boy answered, "Yes, when one wants to steal something." When asked to describe such an occasion, he said, "For example, when I am alone at home and there is some fruit and my father and mother have gone out without giving me any. Then I get to thinking how I should like to take some. But then I think about something else because I don't mean to steal." When asked whether he was always stronger than these thoughts, he said yes, he had never stolen anything. "What do you do when the wish is very strong?" "I still don't take anything," he said triumphantly, "for then I am afraid of my father."

You observe that his superego has reached a considerable degree of independence, which was expressed in his own wish not to be a thief. But when the temptation was too strong, he had to call to his aid the support of the person to whom this wish owed its existence, namely, the father who was the instigator of the warnings and threats of punishment. Another child in the same situation would perhaps have called to mind his love for his mother.

This weakness and dependence of the child's superego demands accord well with another observation, which can be confirmed any number of times: the child has a double set of morals, one for the grown-up world and one for himself and his contemporaries. We know, for example, that at a certain age a child begins to feel shame, i.e., he avoids showing himself naked, or performing his excretory functions in the presence of strange adults and later even in that of his close relatives. But we also know that the same child will undress without any shame before other children, and often will have pleasure from going to the toilet with them. Furthermore, we can observe that a child will experience disgust at certain matters only in the presence of adults—under their pressure, as it were—but when alone or in the company of other children, no such reaction occurs.

I remember a 10-year-old boy who on a walk suddenly pointed to a cow-pat and exclaimed with interest, "Look, how funny that is!" The next moment he realized his mistake and blushed. Later he excused himself, saying that at first he had not realized what it was or he would never have mentioned it. But I know that the same boy, with his friends, will talk about the excretory functions with amusement and without embarrassment. He also reported in analysis that when he is alone he can touch his own excrement with his hand without any particular feeling, but when an adult is present, he finds it very difficult even to mention it.

Shame and disgust are important reaction formations designed to restrain the child's anal and exhibitionistic impulses from breaking through to gratification; but even when they already are fully established, their maintenance and efficacy seem to depend upon the relationship with the adult object.

With these observations on the dependency of the child's superego and his double morals in relation to shame and disgust, we have arrived at the most important difference between the analysis of children and adults. The analysis of a child is by no means an entirely private affair, played out exclusively between two persons, the analyst and his patient. Insofar as the childish superego has not yet become the impersonal representative of the demands taken over from the outer world, and is still organically connected with it—to that extent the relevant external objects play an important role in the analysis itself. This is especially true for its last phase when the instinctual impulses which have been freed from repression must be channeled in new directions.

Let us resume once more the comparison with the adult neurotic. We said that in his analysis we had to reckon only with his instinctual life, his ego, and his superego; in favorable cases, we need not trouble ourselves with the fate of the impulses which have emerged from the unconscious. These come under the influence of his superego, which bears the responsibility for their further employment.

But who bears this responsibility in a child's analysis? To remain consistent, we would have to say: the responsibility should rest with the persons concerned with the child's upbringing, with whom the child's superego is in any case still inseparably bound up, that is, with his parents.

But here we have some serious reservations. We cannot forget that it was these same parents or guardians whose excessive demands drove the child into an excess of repression and into neurosis. The parents who are now called upon to help in the child's recovery are still the same people who let the child get ill in the first place. Their outlook has in most cases not been changed. Only in the most favorable instances have they learned enough from the child's illness to be ready to mitigate their demands. Thus it seems dangerous to leave the decision about the fate of the newly liberated instinctual life entirely in their hands. There is too great a risk that the child will be forced once more into the path of repression and neurosis. In such circumstances it would have been more economical to have omitted altogether the wearisome and painful process of liberation by analysis.

Another consideration needs to be taken into account here. In the case of the adult, there is a long interval between the time he originally developed his neurosis and the time when analysis freed him of it. Between these two points in time he has undergone and completed his entire ego development, so that the being who made the original choice can hardly be called the same person as he who undertakes its revision. But the same does not apply to the child patient whose neurosis may have developed rather recently.

In view of these factors, how can we prematurely declare the child to be of age and expect him to make the important decision how to deal with the impulses now placed at his disposal once more? It is difficult to imagine what would enable him to find his way through the problems in front of him: on which moral precepts should he rely and by which criteria would he evaluate the existing external conditions? I believe that, left alone and with every external support withdrawn, the child can take only a single, short, and convenient path—that toward direct gratification. We know from analytic theory and practice, however, that it is desirable to avoid too much direct gratification of a child's necessarily perverse sexuality at any stage of his development. Otherwise the fixation on the once-experienced pleasure will prove to be a hindrance to further normal development, and the urge for its revival a dangerous incentive to regression from later stages.

It seems to me that there remains but one solution for this difficult situation. The analyst must claim for himself the liberty to guide the child at this important point, in order to secure, to some extent, the achievements of analysis. Under his influence the child must learn how to deal with his instinctual life; the analyst's views must in the end determine what part of the infantile sexual impulses must be suppressed or rejected as unsuitable in civilized society; how much or how little can be allowed direct gratification; and what outlets can be opened up via sublimation.

We may say in short: *the analyst must succeed in putting himself in the place of the child's ego ideal for the duration of the analysis*; he ought not to begin his analytic work of liberation until he has made sure that the child is eager to follow his lead. For this purpose it is essential that the analyst have the position of authority about which we spoke at the beginning. Before the child can give the highest place in his emotional life, that of ego ideal, to this new love object which ranks with the parents, he needs to feel that the analyst's authority is even greater than theirs.

If the child's parents have learned something from his illness, and show an inclination to conform to the analyst's requirements, a real division of analytic and educational labor between home and analyst becomes possible—or rather a cooperation between the two. The child's education suffers no interruption even at the termination of the analysis, but passes back, wholly and directly, from the hands of the analyst into those of the now more understanding parents.

On the other hand, the parents may use their influence to work against the analyst. Since the child is emotionally attached to both, the result is a situation similar to that in an unhappy marriage where the child has become an object of contention. We then cannot be surprised to witness the occurrence of all the injurious consequences for the formation of character with which we are familiar from this other arena. As the child plays off father against mother, he may play off analyst against home, and use the conflicts existing between them as a means to escape from all demands in both cases.

The situation also becomes dangerous when the child, in a phase of resistance, induces in the parents such a negative attitude toward the analysis that they will break off the treatment. Then we lose the child at the very worst moment, in a state of resistance and negative transference, and can be sure that he will exploit in the most undesirable ways what the analysis has liberated in him. Today I would no longer undertake the analysis of a child if the personalities of the parents, or their analytic understanding, did not provide a guarantee against such an outcome.

I will give one last example to illustrate how necessary it is for the analyst to be in control of the relationship between the child's ego and his instincts.

After I had brought my young obsessional patient to the point of allowing her "devil" to speak, she began to com-

municate to me a large number of anal fantasies, hesitatingly at first, but soon with ever-increasing boldness and
detail when she realized that no expressions of displeasure
on my part were forthcoming. Gradually the analytic hour
was entirely given over to anal confidences, and became the
repository of all the daydreams of this kind which otherwise oppressed her. While she talked in this way with me
the constant oppression was relieved. She herself called the
time with me her "rest hour." She once said, "My time
with you, Anna Freud, is my rest hour. I don't have to restrain my devil. But no," she went on, "I have another rest
period, when I am asleep." Apparently during analysis and
sleep she was free of what would be equivalent to the
adult's constant expenditure of energy in maintaining repression. Her relief showed itself above all in an altered,
attentive, and animated manner.

After a time she went a step further. She began to display something of her hitherto strictly guarded anal fantasies and ideas at home as well; for example, when a dish
was brought to the table, she made a half-audible comparison or a "dirty" joke to the other children. I was asked by
the adults what to do about this. Inexperienced as I was, I
took the situation lightly, advising that one should neither
acquiesce in nor reject such minor misbehavior but simply
let it pass unnoticed. The effect was unexpected.

In the absence of external condemnation, the child lost
all moderation, carried over into her home all the ideas previously expressed only during analysis, and completely
revelled, as she had with me, in her anal preoccupations,
comparisons, and expressions. The other members of the
household soon found this intolerable; especially on account of the child's behavior at the dinner table, they lost

all appetite and one after another, children as well as adults, left the room in silent disapproval. My little patient had behaved like a pervert or a mentally ill adult, and thereby put herself beyond the pale of society. Since she was not punished by being removed from the company of others, the consequence was that they removed themselves from her. During this period she abandoned all restraints in other respects as well. In a few days she had become transformed into a cheerful, insolent, and disobedient child, by no means dissatisfied with herself.

The adults returned to me to complain. They said the state of affairs was unendurable. What ought they to do? Should they tell the child that talking of such things was not in itself wicked, but ask her to give it up at home for their sake? I did not agree to this suggestion. I had to acknowledge that I had made a mistake, in crediting the child's superego with an independent inhibitory strength which it did not possess. As soon as the important people in the external world had relaxed their demands, the child's superego, previously strict and strong enough to bring forth a whole series of obsessional symptoms, suddenly had turned compliant. My relying on the obsessional structure had been incautious and had not even furthered the analysis itself. I had changed an inhibited, obsessional child into one whose "perverse" tendencies were liberated. But, in doing so, I had also ruined the situation for my work. This liberated child now had her "rest hour" all day long, lost her enthusiasm for our joint work to a considerable degree, and no longer brought me the proper material because this was now spread over the whole day instead of being reserved for the analytic session; moreover, she had temporarily lost insight that anything was wrong with her and needed help. The classical maxim that the analytic work can be carried out only in a state of abstinence has even greater application to the analysis of children than to that of adults.

Fortunately, the situation was not so bad as it looked and in practice was easy to solve. I asked the family to do nothing except have patience. I would deal with the child's behavior but could not promise how soon the result would show. In the child's next session I acted energetically; I said all this was a breach of our agreement; I had thought she had wanted to tell me about these dirty matters in order to be rid of them, but now I saw that this was by no means so, that she wanted to tell them to everybody, for the pleasure of doing so. I had nothing against that, but in that case I could not see that she needed me; we could simply give up our hours together and let her have her pleasure. But if she stuck to her first intention, she must tell these things only to me and to no one else. The more she kept to herself at home, the more would occur to her during her hour; and the more I would know about her, the easier it would be to rid her of it. She must now decide and choose.

She went very pale and reflected for some time, and then looked at me and said, with the same thoughtful comprehension as on the first occasion, "If you say that that is how it is, I will not talk like that anymore." With that her obsessional conscientiousness returned. From that day on no mention of the objectionable topic crossed her lips at home. She was retransformed, but she had again turned from a naughty and perverted child into an inhibited and apathetic one.

We had to accomplish similar transformations several

more times in the course of her treatment. Whenever the analytic work succeeded in liberating her from her unusually severe obsessional neurosis, she always escaped to the other extreme; then all I could do was once again to restore the neurosis and the already vanished "devil" to his place; naturally each time this occurred with diminished intensity and I used greater precautions and gentleness than had been used in her previous upbringing. Finally we succeeded in getting her to steer a middle course between the two extremes.

I would not have enlarged upon this example if it did not serve to illustrate all the characteristics of the analysis of children put forward in this last section: the fact that a child's superego is weak; that his superego demands and consequently his neurosis are dependent on the external world; that the child himself is incapable of controlling the instincts that have been freed; and that for this reason the analyst must take charge and guide them.[1] The analyst accordingly combines in his own person two difficult and diametrically opposed functions: he has to analyze and educate, that is to say, in the same breath he must allow and forbid, loosen and bind again. If the analyst does not succeed in this, analysis may become the child's charter for all the ill conduct prohibited by society. But if the analyst succeeds, he undoes a piece of wrong education and abnormal development, and so procures for the child, and whoever controls his destiny, another opportunity to improve matters.

[1] To be in-charge of this guidance offers the child analyst other advantages as well. It makes the application of Ferenczi's "active therapy" possible, the suppression of individual symptoms, which then leads to the damming up of libido, which in turn should make more abundant material available for the analysis.

You know that when we terminate the analysis of an adult, we do not compel him to become healthy. It is entirely his decision what to do with the new opportunities that are now open to him; whether he once more will take the path into neurosis, whether his ego development will permit his taking the opposite direction toward extensive instinctual gratification, or whether he will achieve a compromise between the two, a real synthesis of the conflicting forces within him.

Nor can we force the parents of our small patients to take a reasonable course with the child who has once again been returned to them. The analysis of children is no insurance against all the harm which the child's future may hold for him. It works above all on the past; but thereby it provides a cleared and improved ground for future development.

From the conditions which I have described you will have gleaned an important clue as to the indications for the analysis of children. These indications are not determined solely by the fact that the child suffers from a specific illness. The analysis of children belongs essentially in the analytic milieu, and for the present will probably have to be confined to the children of analysts or of people who have been analyzed or regard analysis with a certain confidence and respect. Only in this way can the transition from the analytic education in the course of treatment back to education in the parental home be accomplished without a break. Where a child's analysis cannot be organically grafted onto the rest of his life, but intrudes into his other relationships like a foreign body and interferes with them, it probably will create more conflicts for the child than can be resolved by the treatment.

These statements, too, I am afraid, will disappoint those

among you who were quite ready to show some confidence in child analysis.

But after telling you so much about the limitations of the analysis of children, I should not like to close without saying something of the considerable possibilities which child analysis, in spite of all its difficulties, seems to me to hold out and which in some respects may even have an advantage over adult analysis. I can see primarily three such possibilities.

We can bring about quite different modifications of character in the child than in the adult. The child who under the influence of his neurosis has started out on the path of an abnormal character development need only retrace his steps a short distance in order to find again the road which is normal and appropriate to his natural tendencies. Unlike the adult, he has not yet built up his whole life, made his professional choice, formed friendships and love relationships—all on the basis of his abnormal development which has influenced his ego and his identifications and in turn shaped his character and neurosis. In the "character analysis" of an adult we must actually shatter his whole life and achieve the virtually impossible, that is to say: undo actions already done, and not only make their consequences conscious but abolish them altogether if we wish for real success. Here the analysis of children has an infinite advantage over that of adults.

The second possibility concerns the influence upon the superego. The moderation of its severity is, as you know, one of the aims of analyzing neuroses. But in this respect the analysis of adults encounters the greatest difficulties because it has to contend with the individual's oldest and most significant love objects, his parents, whom he has introjected through identification, and who in his memory are further protected by filial piety. But in the child, as you have seen, we are dealing with living persons, existing in the real world and not enshrined in memory. When we supplement internal work by external, and seek to modify, not only the existing identifications by analyzing them, but their actual prototypes by exerting ordinary influence, the result is both impressive and surprising.

The same is true for the third point. In working with an adult we have to confine ourselves entirely to his own attempts to deal with his environment. We would never make attempts, which are in any case beyond our intentions and our power, to shape his surroundings to meet his needs. But with a child we can do just this without any great difficulty. A child's needs are simpler and easier to recognize and to fulfill; our powers, combined with those of the parents, easily suffice under favorable conditions to provide for the child just what he requires, or much of it, at every stage of his treatment and progressive development. Thus we lighten the child's task of adaptation as we endeavor to adjust his surroundings to him. Here again we need to perform double work, from within and from without.

I believe that it is due to these three factors that in the analysis of children, in spite of all the difficulties I have recounted, we can aim at transformations, improvements, and recoveries which we could not even dream of in the analysis of adults.

Ladies and Gentlemen! I am prepared for the practicing analysts among you to say, after what they have heard here, that my methods with children are so different that they cannot be called real analysis at all, but are a form of "wild" analysis which has borrowed all its tools from analysis but in no way conforms to strict analytic principles. But consider: if an adult neurotic came to your consulting room to ask for treatment, and on closer examination proved as impulsive, as undeveloped intellectually, and as deeply dependent on his environment as are my child patients, you would probably say, "Freudian analysis is a fine method, but it is not designed for such people." And you would treat the patient by a mixed method, giving him as much pure analysis as he can stand and for the rest child analysis —because, owing to his infantile nature, he would merit nothing better.

In my opinion, it is no reflection on the analytic method, designed as it is for a single particular object, the adult neurotic, if one seeks to apply it with modifications to other types of objects. There is no harm in contriving to use it for other purposes. Only one should be at pains to know what one is doing.

Part II

FOUR LECTURES ON PSYCHO-ANALYSIS FOR TEACHERS AND PARENTS (1930)

See pp. xviiff. for publishing history of this book.
The version presented here has been revised by the author.

Infantile Amnesia and the Oedipus Complex

We are all aware that teachers are still very suspicious and doubtful of psychoanalysis. When, therefore, in spite of this, you as teachers working at the Day Care Centers[1] of the City of Vienna decided to have a short course of lectures from me, you must somehow or other have received

[1] The German *Hort* is here translated as "day care center." A quotation from an account of a *Hort* reads: "*Horts* are designed on the model of nursery schools, but particularly planned for children from 6 to 14 years of age. While nursery schools only take children up to 6 years, i.e., until school age, the children who come to *Horts* are those whose parents go out to work and who would have to resort to the streets after school hours. Here, in the *Hort*, they prepare their school homework, occupy themselves with communal games, and are taken for outings."

the impression that a closer acquaintance with this new discipline might be able to afford you some help in your difficult work. After you have listened to the four lectures, you will be able to decide whether you were mistaken in your expectation, or whether I have been able to fulfill at least some of your hopes.

In one particular direction I have certainly nothing new to offer you. I should fail in my object if I attempted to tell you anything about the behavior of schoolchildren or day care children, since you are in this respect in the more advantageous position. An immense amount of material passes through your hands in your daily work, and demonstrates very clearly the whole range of the phenomena before you: from the physically and mentally retarded children, the obstinate, cowed, lying, and ill-treated children, to the brutal, aggressive, and delinquent ones. I prefer not to attempt to give you a complete list, for whatever I do you might well point out to me a large number of omissions.

Nevertheless, the very situation that gives you such a complete knowledge of these phenomena has its drawbacks. As workers in day care—or as teachers in the schools and in the nursery schools—you are obliged ceaselessly to *act*. The life and movement in your classes or groups demand constant interference on your part; you have to admonish, to discipline, to keep order, to occupy, to advise, and to instruct the children. The authorities above you would be greatly dissatisfied if it suddenly occurred to you to withdraw to the position of passive observer. Thus it comes about that in the practice of your profession you become acquainted with innumerable visible manifestations of childish behavior, but you are unable to arrange systematically the phenomena before your eyes, nor can you trace to their original source the children's behavior to which you are bound to react.

Perhaps even more than the opportunity for undisturbed observation you lack the power to make a correct classification and explanation of the material in your possession, for such classification requires very specialized knowledge. Let us assume for the moment that one among this audience is especially interested in finding out why certain children in a particular group suffer from inflamed eyes or rickets. He knows that these children come from miserable, damp homes, but only medical knowledge can explain clearly to him the special way in which the dampness of the walls at home leads to the child's physical defect. Another of you, perhaps, concentrates his attention on the dangers to which the children of alcoholics are exposed owing to innate factors; in this case he needs to turn to the study of heredity. Whoever wishes to discover the connection between unemployment, the housing shortage, and child neglect needs to read up on sociology. Similarly, the teacher who desires to learn more of the mental background of all the phenomena which I have listed above, who would like to understand the differences between them and follow their gradual development in the case of the individual child, may turn for information to the new science of psychoanalysis.

Any such assistance in practical work through increased knowledge seems to me of special importance to day care workers. There are two reasons for this. The Day Center is the newest of the educational institutions of the City of Vienna. It is intended for all children who for internal or external reasons are not under parental care after school hours. The Day Center is conceived as a preventive measure to counteract the growing neglect of children. It owes its existence to the conviction that in the earlier stages of wayward and antisocial behavior it is comparatively easy to exert a beneficial influence in the relaxed atmosphere of such centers, which resemble, yet are unlike, the school or parental environment. It is much more difficult to do this later when the long-neglected or criminal adolescents are isolated in reformatories and are then too often beyond any educational attempts.

Nevertheless, at present attendance at a day care center cannot be enforced. While the authorities can compel the parents to send their children to schools, it is for the time being left to the parents' own judgment whether they wish to entrust to day care a child to whom they themselves can offer only the worst conditions at home. For this reason the day care centers must constantly justify their existence to each child and to each of his parents by especially successful work, just as before the introduction of compulsory vaccination, parents had again and again to be convinced of the necessity for inoculation.

But day care workers encounter another special difficulty that is inherent in their position. They have to deal almost exclusively with children who have already had a whole series of more or less upsetting experiences and who have already passed through the hands of various educators. They are bound to notice that these children, at any rate at first, do not react to them as the people that they are, nor to their actual behavior. Instead, they bring with them a set attitude of mind, and may approach the teacher with the suspicion, defiance, or wariness which they have acquired in their earlier dealings with other adults. Moreover, the life of a child in day care is no more than a supplement to his school life and the day centers generally adopt methods more liberal, humane, and modern than prevail in most schools. Thus it happens that the standard of behavior which the school demands from and inculcates in the children often proves an obstacle to the attainment of the aims of day care.

The position of day care workers is, therefore, by no means enviable. In almost every case they are faced with difficult tasks which require independent action and intervention; and this, quite apart from the fact that they are never the main and most important adults in the children's lives.

Schoolteachers at this point may well complain that we are quite wrong to regard their position as more favorable. They also maintain that they seldom get the child early enough, and that it is very difficult, for example, to accustom the children in the first grade of elementary school to a correct and serious attitude toward the teacher and learning when they have previously known only the playful atmosphere of nursery school. They bring with them into the school the behavior acquired in the kindergarten, an attitude which is no longer suitable to the requirements of school.

Yet when we turn to the nursery school teachers, who, according to the view just expressed, should be in the enviable position of working in untilled ground, we hear to our amazement the complaint that even their 3- to 6-year-old charges are already finished personalities. Each child brings with him his own characteristics, and reacts to the behavior of the teacher in his own specific way. In each child the teacher meets definite expectations, clear patterns of hopes and fears, dislikes and preferences, individual forms of jealousy and tenderness, the need for love or the rejection of it. There is no question of a teacher impressing her own individuality upon a still unformed being. She is moving among complex miniature personalities whom it is by no means easy to influence.

Thus the teachers—whether in day centers, schools, or nursey schools—all find themselves in the same difficult position. The development of human beings is obviously accomplished earlier than is generally imagined. In order to trace to their origins the children's peculiarities which give teachers so much trouble, investigations must extend to the period prior to entrance into the public institutions, they must go back to those adults who were actually the first ones in the child's life, that is, to the period before age 5 and to the parents.

You may have gained the impression that our task is thereby simplified. Instead of observing the daily behavior of the older children in the schools or day centers, we shall seek to gather from them accounts of the impressions and memories of their earliest years.

At first sight this does not appear to be difficult. In all your contacts with the children entrusted to your care you have always tried to establish frank and trusting relations with them. This will now be very useful. The child will be prepared to tell you everything in answer to your questions.

I advise all of you to make this attempt, but I can inform you in advance that it will yield poor results. Children give no information about their past: they willingly talk about the events of the last few days or weeks, about holidays spent elsewhere, about a previous birthday, perhaps even about Christmas of last year. But there their recollections stop, or at any rate they lack the ability to tell about them.

You may say that we were merely too confident in our belief in the child's capacity to remember his past life. We ought to have borne in mind that children do not distinguish between important and unimportant events. It would therefore, you think, be much more reasonable and rewarding to address the inquiry not to the child, but to an adult who is interested in an investigation of the earliest experiences of his childhood.

I certainly advise you to carry out this second plan as well, but I know you will be surprised to find that the friend to whom you apply and who is only too willing to help you also has very little to tell you. His recollections will probably go back, with few gaps and quite intelligently, to his fifth or sixth year. He will describe his schooling, perhaps even the houses where he lived in this third, fourth, or fifth year, the number and names of his brothers and sisters; and he may even mention a specific event such as a move from one house to another, or a particular accident. Then his account will come to an end before you have found what you sought, namely, indications about how his development during those first years proceeded and led to his individual personality with its special characteristics.

Obviously, there is a good reason for this new disappointment. The events we are searching for, which play such an important part in the development of the individual's character, are those which concern the most intimate events in his life. They are experiences which a person guards as his most private concerns, admits only to himself, and hides bashfully even from his closest friends. We should have taken this into account, and applied for data to the only person ready to yield information. That is to say, each investigator must investigate himself. Where we ourselves are concerned, we ought to be able to rely on the capacity of a normal adult to remember the past, to be interested in the inquiry, and on a willingness to overcome all the barriers which prevent a person from revealing his secret life to another.

Nevertheless, even if we do give all our interest and attention to the matter and are as frank as we can be, the results will still be very poor. We shall not succeed in really elucidating the earliest years of our life and in assembling an unbroken series of memories of that period. We may be able to string together incidents up to certain points of time, which differ greatly for different individuals. With some it is the fifth year, with some the fourth, with others the third. Before that period, however, there is for each of us a great blank, a darkness with only isolated and disconnected fragments lighted up, and these on closer inspection seem to have neither meaning nor significance.

A young man, for example, remembers nothing of the first four years of his childhood except a brief scene on a ship where the captain, clad in a beautiful uniform, stretched out his arms to lift him over a little parapet. Yet at that very time he had experienced the stormiest conflicts and the most severe blows of fate—as could be ascertained by questioning other people. Or again, a girl whose early childhood was replete with emotional experiences and many stirring events retained but a single clear recollection: of being taken out in a baby carriage and turning back her head to look at her nanny who was pushing it!

You will grant that here we are up against a startlingly

contradictory set of facts. On the one hand, we know from our observation of little children, and from the accounts which our relatives give us of our own childhood, that the child behaves at this stage intelligently and energetically, shows likes and dislikes, and conducts himself in many important respects quite like a rational being. On the other hand, this period has vanished from his own memory, or at most has left behind it only very incomplete traces. According to the evidence given by the teachers in schools and nursery schools, human beings after the expiration of these very early years step into life as completely formed small individuals. And yet memory acts as if it were not worthwhile to preserve traces of a time in which each child was especially receptive and impressionable, a time when this complex development into an individual personality proceeded.

Academic psychology has so far been deceived by this semblance of things. Since academic psychologists regard as material for their science only that part of mental life which is known to the individual himself, they must necessarily underestimate the significance of the first years of life, which remain unknown to him.

It was psychoanalysis that first tackled this contradiction. Examining the small mistakes in the everyday life of human beings, such as forgetting, losing, or misplacing things, misreading or mishearing, psychoanalysis succeeded in demonstrating that such errors are always based on an intent of the person who makes them. Previously these occurrences had been explained, without much thought, as the results of lack of attention, fatigue, or mere chance. Psychoanalytic investigation established that, generally speaking, we forget nothing except what we wish to forget for some good reason or other, though that reason is usually quite unknown to us.

Similarly, in investigating the gaps in memory for childhood, psychoanalysis does not content itself with the usual means of explanation. It assumes that such a striking phenomenon could not have occurred without some very strong motive. Precisely this obscurity, shrouding the first years of life, and the obstacles in the way of all direct efforts to illuminate them, led psychoanalysts to suspect that something of importance was hidden there. In the same way any burglar meeting an especially elaborate safety lock would conclude that his efforts to crack it will be well rewarded; people would not take so much trouble to lock up something worthless!

But it is not my intention to describe to you now the way in which psychoanalysis has succeeded in its aim of recovering the childhood memories. The description of the psychoanalytic method would in itself claim far more time than we have at our disposal. We must leave a more detailed study and examination of this for another possible course. At present we are chiefly interested in the content of the first years of life so far as psychoanalysis has succeeded in establishing it. I can mention only that this has been accomplished, following the unraveling of the errors and dreams of the healthy as well as the symptoms of neurotic people.

The psychoanalytic reconstruction of childhood extends as far back as earliest infancy, when the child possesses only the inherited characteristics which he brings with him at birth—to that state, in other words, in which we erroneously hoped to find him when he entered our educational institutions. What can be reported about this stage of life is not very impressive. The tiny human being before us is similar to a newborn animal in many respects, though worse off in some ways than the animal young. The latter are dependent on their mothers for only a short period, at most a few weeks. After that they evolve into independent creatures who can manage without further care. It is quite different with human beings.

The child remains for at least a year so completely dependent on his mother that he would perish the moment she withdrew her care. But even after the expiration of this year of infancy, independence is still far away. The child is unable to procure his food, to support himself, and to protect himself against dangers. As we know, the human being needs fifteen years or more before he can completely dispense with the protection of the adults and become an adult individual himself.

This difference between human beings and animals—the child's prolonged period of complete dependence—determines his entire destiny. If during the entire first year of life nothing stands between the child and annihilation except the tender care of his mother, we cannot be surprised to learn that the maintenance of this tie to the mother assumes a very important role in his life. The little child feels safe as long as he knows his mother is near at hand, and he shows his helplessness by outbreaks of anxiety when she leaves him. He needs his mother for the satisfaction of his hunger; she becomes a necessity of life.

But the relationship between infant and mother soon extends far beyond what can be explained as a striving for the preservation of life. We observe that the child wants his mother near him and longs for her even when his hunger is satisfied and no special dangers are threatening. We say the child loves his mother. In response to her tender love and care a bond with his mother has been established within him. It is true that this bond coincides with the instinct for self-preservation on which it is based; nevertheless it has become independent of this instinct and goes far beyond it.

The tender relationship between infant and mother seems to offer every chance for a peaceful physical and mental development. And certainly, the young child would be completely content if his mother did nothing but feed him, take care of him, and love him.

But now comes the moment when for the first time the external world enters as a disturbing factor into this relationship. The child who has now left infancy and the first year behind him begins to realize that his mother does not belong to him exclusively. The family of which he is only a small and not a very important part has other members—father and brothers and sisters, of whose presence he has only just become aware, but who appear to be just as important as he deems himself to be. They all, indeed, assert a right to the possession of the mother.

It can easily be understood that the small child regards his brothers and sisters as his enemies. He is jealous of them and wishes them out of the way so as to restore the original state of affairs, which alone is satisfactory to him.

You can convince yourselves of this jealousy in little children by observing their behavior, for example, at the birth of another child. Thus a little 2-year-old girl, whose father proudly showed her the newly born brother—expecting her to feel joy and admiration—merely asked, "When will he die again?" A mother told me that when she was feeding her infant at the breast, her 3-year-old boy, armed with a stick or some other pointed object, would come quite close to her, and that she had great difficulty in preventing him from doing harm to the baby. This type of occurrence can be multiplied endlessly. As a matter of fact, one hears of serious injuries which children 2 and 3 years old inflict on their younger brothers or sisters if they are unwisely left alone with them.

We have every reason to regard this jealousy of small children as serious. It springs from the same motives as the jealousy of adults, and causes the child the same amount of suffering as we endure in adult life when our relation to a beloved person is disturbed by unwelcome rivals. The only difference is that the child is more restricted in his actions than the adult, and thus the satisfaction of his jealous feelings goes no further than a wish. He wishes the tiresome brothers and sisters to go away, he would like them to be dead. To the little child who has not yet learned to grasp the meaning of death there is as yet no difference between going away and being dead.

This wish for his brothers and sisters to be dead is thoroughly natural on the part of the child. The more the child values the possession of his mother, the more violent is this desire. The child, moreover, is at first completely single-minded in his hostile feelings. An emotional conflict arises within him only when he realizes that his mother, who inexplicably loves these disturbing brothers and sisters, demands that he give up these evil wishes, share the mother with them, and even love them. Here is the starting point of all the difficulties in the emotional relations among children within a family.

You probably know from your own observation of older children how frequently the notion of "brotherly love"

represents only the adult's wishful thinking, and how different the real relationships between siblings are from what
the parents would like them to be. It is, moreover, a striking proof of the correctness of the situation here described
that the jealousy between brothers and sisters is much less
intense where the relationship with the mother is less close.
In underprivileged families, where a working mother is unable to devote as much time and care to her children, the
loss of tenderness at the birth of a younger sibling is cor-
respondingly smaller. For this reason one often finds in
these families more love and sympathy between siblings
than in the well-to-do middle class. In the latter each child
sees his brothers and sisters as rivals for a very real possession, and accordingly hatred and jealousy, open or hidden,
dominate the situation.

However, the turmoil of feelings which the little child
experiences in relation to his siblings is relatively harmless
compared with another, more powerful emotional conflict.
Siblings are not the only rivals who compete with the child
for possession of the mother: the father is far more important in this respect. It is the father who plays a double
role in the little child's life. He is hated as a rival when he
claims ownership of the mother, takes her away, goes out
with her, treats her as his property, and insists upon sleeping with her by himself. But he is also loved and admired
by the child who relies on his help, believes in his strength
and omnipotence, and has no greater desire than to be like
him in the future. Thus for the little boy there arises the
extraordinary and at first quite insoluble problem that he
loves and admires the same person whom he also hates and
wishes to be dead. In relation to his siblings it was only a
question of restraining his evil wishes in order to please his

mother. In relation to the father, for the first time two opposite feelings are in direct conflict with each other. I leave it to you to imagine for yourselves the further difficulties into which the little boy is plunged by this conflict: the fear of the power of his evil wishes, of his father's revenge and the loss of his love, the destruction of all ease and innocence in his relations with his mother, his bad conscience, and his fear of death. I shall have more to say about this in another place.

You probably feel that it may be interesting to pursue the history of the young child's emotional development, but that you do not see how this is related to your own particular work. You think that the much older children with whom you deal have long outgrown the stage of complete dependence on the mother, the early jealousy, and all those stormy conflicts of the first years of life. But in this you are mistaken. What you meet in your groups or classes are phenomena directly connected with this earlier period of life. The children whom you call quarrelsome, asocial, envious, and discontent are substituting their schoolmates for their siblings, and there, at school, are fighting out with them conflicts which have remained unsolved at home. Similarly, those who react violently if you exercise the slightest show of authority, or those who are so cowed that they do not even venture to look you in the face or to raise their voices in class, have substituted you for their father and transferred to you either the hostility and death wishes toward him or the rejection of such wishes, with the resultant anxious submissiveness. You get here the explanation of a phenomenon which formerly surprised you. It is quite true that at age 6, children bring with them their prescribed reactions, and that they merely repeat them in relation to you. What you see being enacted before your eyes are really only repetitions and new editions of very old conflicts of which you are the target but not the cause.

I anticipate a second objection from you. You probably maintain that the family as I have depicted it does not exist at all, at least not in the case of most of the children with whom you have to deal. You very rarely find a mother who bestows on her children such loving care and tenderness and distributes it so impartially. Nor do you often find a father who lives with his wife on such friendly terms and is at the same time qualified to be the object of the love and admiration of his little son. The picture is as a rule quite different.

But I had a quite definite intention in mind when describing this model family. I wanted to impress you with the difficult position in which the child finds himself due to his conflicting emotions even in the most favorable external circumstances. Each factor that contributes to a worsening of the external conditions—that is to say, anything that casts a shadow over the picture of the model family life—will at the same time intensify the conflict within the child.

Let us assume that the child is not brought up by his own mother at all, but during this most important first year of his life is placed with one foster family after another, or is taken care of in an institution by more or less indifferent and changing nurses. Ought we not to assume that the lack of this first natural emotional bond will greatly influence his later life?

Or let us assume that the father whom the boy takes as his model and in whose footsteps he seeks to follow is an alcoholic, or psychotic, or a criminal. In this case the striving to become like the father, which normally is one of the greatest aids in education, leads to the direct ruin of the child.

When the parents are separated and each parent tries to win over the child to his or her side and to represent the other as the guilty party, then the entire emotional development of the child is at risk. His confidence is shattered as his critical powers are awakened prematurely.

I will quote here the pronouncement of an 8-year-old boy who made vain efforts to bring his divorcing parents together again. He said: "If my father does not love my mother, then my mother does not love my father, and then they can't like me either. Then I don't like them. And then the whole family is rotten." The conclusions which a child draws from such a state of affairs are generally dangerous. He acts like an employee in a bankrupt firm who has lost all confidence in his principals and therefore no longer has any interest in carrying out his tasks. In such circumstances the child also ceases to fulfill his task, i.e., his normal development, and he reacts to the abnormal conditions by developing some abnormality.

Ladies and gentlemen, enough for today. What I have placed before you are the events of the first years of childhood in the way in which they have been reconstructed with the psychoanalytic method. I do not know how far the details appear to you believable or improbable. In any case, these discoveries of psychoanalysis have helped to direct the attention of people in general to the significance of the earliest years of life.

In conclusion, I present to you a case which illustrates the practical consequences of such theoretical considerations.

A little while ago a German court of law had to pronounce judgment in a divorce case. In the course of the lawsuit the question arose to which of the parents the 2-year-old child should be assigned. The lawyer appearing for the husband proved that the wife, on account of a whole series of character traits, was not properly qualified to educate the child. To this the wife's lawyer objected, maintaining that a child in his second year merely needed care, not yet education. In order to decide the issue the opinion of experts was taken as to the point in time when a child's education might be said to begin. The experts who were called belonged only partly to the psychoanalytic school, partly to other and more orthodox scientific factions. Nevertheless they unanimously agreed that *the education of a child begins with the first day of life.*

We have every reason to assume that prior to the discoveries of psychoanalysis the experts would have decided otherwise.

2

The Instinctual Life of
Early Childhood

I am uncertain how you took what I said in my last lecture, but I venture to surmise that the impression left on you was a twofold one. For one, you probably think that I have presented nothing but facts already well known to you, and that I have done this with much unnecessary emphasis; that I falsely assume that we are still at the stage where teachers regarded their pupils as units apart from their families; that I forget that today even the youngest teacher, when meeting difficulties, thinks first of all of the child's home environment, of unfavorable parental influences, of the effects produced in the child by being either the eldest or the youngest or the middle child in the family. You always try to explain the child's conduct at school by the way he is treated at home. Thus, long before I lectured to you, you were aware of the fact that the child's character is greatly influenced by experiences in the home.

On the other hand, you may feel that I have exaggerated what is in reality simple by interpreting the feelings and acts of little children in analogy with the corresponding manifestations of adults. Thus I have converted the ordinary friction of the child with his brothers and sisters into serious death wishes; and the quite innocent and tender relation of the boy to his mother into the love of a man who desires a woman sexually.

To you it appears quite natural that the boy in his daily relations with his father realizes the latter's superior power, and submits unwillingly to paternal commands which restrict his freedom. But as I see it, the conflict between father and son takes on the magnitude of a struggle to the death. You had already heard with astonishment the report that psychoanalysis went so far as to compare the emotional situation of the little child with that of King Oedipus of the Greek myth who slew his father and possessed his mother. Perhaps I have simply proved to you by my presentation that the prejudice which you had always felt toward psychoanalysis was not unfounded, and what was prejudice before is now a considered opinion on the ground of your own experience. At this point I do not want to defend the psychoanalytic viewpoint with further arguments. I ask you merely to suspend judgment for a little while.

Let us return once more to the verdict given by the German law court, which, as I have pointed out to you, is in complete agreement with psychoanalysis. What should we conceive of as "education" from the first day of life? What is there, indeed, to educate in the tiny animallike creature, of whose mental processes we have hitherto known so little? Where can an educational effort take hold? According to the description I have sketched of the child's inner life and of his relations to the people of his environment, one might perhaps think the answer was simple. The task would be to check the hostile wishes directed toward siblings and father, as well as the wish for sexual possession of the mother, and to prevent them from materializing.

But on closer consideration this definition of early education appears unsatisfactory and somewhat ridiculous. The young child stands helpless and powerless amid his environment. We know that he is kept alive only by the kindness of those around him. Every comparison of his strength with theirs is very much to his disadvantage. He has, thus, not the slightest chance of carrying out his dangerous wishes. It is true that in the juvenile courts and children's clinics there are cases in which boys have actually taken over the sexual role of the father toward the mother as far as their physical development permits, or in which a little girl has been used by her own father for sexual purposes. But in all such cases it is never the strength and energy of the child that effects this abnormal fulfillment of his emotional wishes, but the abnormal behavior of the adults who exploit the child's wishes for the satisfaction of their own lusts. In actual life it is as a rule far more important to protect the child from the father's violence than the father from the child's hostility.

Thus the question of how to define education at the beginning of life is still unsolved, and we know little about its purport. Perhaps we can get a new starting point for answering it if—again in reference to the legal verdict quoted above—we compare the two ideas of child care and child education.

There is no difficulty about a definition of child care. The rearing of the child consists of the fulfillment of his bodily needs. Whoever takes care of the child satisfies his hunger, keeps him clean—though the latter is probably more in response to the adult's desire than the child's—sees he is warm and comfortable, and protects him against troubles and dangers. The child is given all he needs without anything being asked in return. Education, in contrast, always demands something of the child.

It would lead me far beyond my own province if I were to begin to describe to you the innumerable past and present aims of education. The adults to whom the child belongs always want to make of him what suits them, i.e., they have aims which differ according to the century, position, class, political affiliation, etc., of the adults. Nevertheless, these various aims have one feature in common. The universal tendency of education is always to turn the child into a grown-up person not very different from the adult world around him. Consequently, we may consider as the starting point for education that it sets in wherever the child differs from the adult, i.e., it struggles with the child's demeanor, or as the adults see it: his misdemeanors.

It would be a mistake for me to spare you the recital of these on the ground that every teacher and child care worker knows them from his own observation. But what the child reveals in school only faintly reflects what is within him. A true description of these characteristics could be obtained only from those who live in close contact with him from infancy to age 5. When we question such people we hear something like this: children are frightfully inconsiderate and egotistic; they are concerned only with getting their own way and satisfying their own wishes whether this hurts others or not. They are dirty and messy; they do not mind touching the most disgusting matters or even putting them to the mouth. They are quite shameless so far as their own body is concerned and very curious about the things that other people wish to conceal from them. They are greedy and crave sweets. They are cruel to all living creatures that are weaker than they themselves and take great pleasure in destroying inanimate objects. They engage in an abundance of bad habits as far as the body is concerned: they suck their fingers, bite their nails, pick their noses, and play with their sexual organs; and they do all these things with intense passion, bent on gratifying every one of their wishes, and are quite intolerant of even the slightest postponement.

There are two chief complaints raised by parents. One is a feeling of hopelessness; scarcely have they broken the child of one bad habit than another takes its place. The other is a sense of bewilderment. They cannot understand where all this comes from. Certainly not from the parents' examples; and they have been careful to keep their own child away from contact with children known to be depraved.

You will say that this account of childish attributes is an indictment rather than an objective description. But, then, adults have never taken an objective attitude to children's characteristics. Instead of observing them, they have acted throughout the centuries somewhat like severe teachers who approach the investigation of every incident among their pupils with anger and indignation. They will never succeed in obtaining the real facts of a case and tracing it back to its source if they do not learn to postpone judgment until the end of their investigation. Until then, what appears to them as the "misdemeanors" of children will remain merely a chaotic, disorderly mass of peculiarities. There is nothing to be done except to lament it!

Moreover, until now, even the scientific observers have not regarded the child in a much more objective light. They adopted the expedient of denying all those features which did not fit into the picture which, working from quite other hypotheses, they had drawn of the child's nature. It was psychoanalysis that first freed itself from the judgments, the assumptions, and the prejudices with which adults have from time immemorial approached the evaluation of infantile nature.

As a result, the mass of inexplicable and displeasing phenomena arranged itself into an organic whole. What had appeared as arbitrary peculiarities was shown to be an orderly sequence of developmental stages such as have been long recognized for the growth of the human body. Psychoanalysis also found the answer to the parents' two complaints mentioned above. Neither the rapid replacement of one habit by another nor their arousal without external influence remain puzzling once these habits are no longer seen as deplorable, haphazard abnormalities, but are viewed as natural, normal links in an organic chain of development.

The first indication of such an orderly sequence was the observation that the choice of the body areas which play a part in the child's habits is not an arbitrary one but is predetermined. You may remember that in our first talk we traced the close emotional tie between infant and mother to the first nourishment and care given to the child by the mother. The first "habit" of the child arises from the same cause and is located at the same place.

In the first weeks of the child's existence food plays the most important role in his life; and at this time his mouth and the area connected with it are the most important parts of his body. Sucking at his mother's breast and milk flowing into his mouth are very pleasant for the child, who then retains the wish for the continuation and repetition of this sensual experience even when he has satisfied his hunger. He soon learns how to reproduce these pleasurable sensations, independently of food intake and of the person who suckles him, by sucking his own finger. Then we say the child "sucks." His face as he does this has the same contented expression as when his mother is suckling him, and consequently the motive for sucking was never really in doubt: the child sucks because he enjoys sucking. The pleasure gained from sucking, which was originally only a by-product of food intake, has made itself independent of it and has become an activity which the child enjoys. In contrast, the adult world has always objected to pleasure sucking and regarded it as a "bad habit."

Moreover, the pleasure-giving activity of the mouth is by no means confined to food intake and finger sucking. The child acts as if he would like to become acquainted with the whole world within his reach by means of his mouth. He bites, he licks and tastes everything near him. Those who take care of him disapprove of such behavior which they regard as "unhygienic," i.e., a danger to health. The preeminent part played by the mouth as the source of pleasurable experience lasts more or less during the whole of the first year of life, with its derivatives persisting into far later ages and stages. I refer here to the aforementioned greediness and the craving for sweets.

The next body zone to come into the foreground and assume the significant place formerly held by the mouth is also codetermined by external experiences. Until this time the grown-up world has been very tolerant toward the child, has in fact devoted itself almost entirely to caring for him, the only exceptions being the demand that he become accustomed to some order and regularity in taking his food and going to sleep. But now a very important factor gradually enters into the child's life—training in cleanliness. His mother or nurse endeavor to break him of wetting and dirtying himself. It is not easy to teach the child to control these functions. Indeed, one can say that the whole second year of life proceeds under the impact of these frequently very energetic efforts on the part of the adults to inculcate cleanliness.

I expect you feel that the child cannot be blamed for the length of time it takes to achieve toilet training. His sphincter muscles may not yet be sufficiently developed to enable him to retain his urine and regulate his movements. I agree that this is correct so far as the earliest period is concerned; but later it is otherwise. Close observation of the child makes one suspect that, though he is no longer unable to control the sphincters, he is protecting his right to eject his excreta when it pleases him, and that he treats the products of his body as his very own. He begins to show extraordinary interest in his own feces; he tries to touch them, to play with them, and, indeed, if he is not prevented, will even put them into his mouth. Here again, we can without difficulty guess the motive for his behavior from the expression on his face and the ardor with which he pursues it. They obviously delight the child, they are pleasurable.

The significant point is that this pleasure is no longer connected with the strength or weakness of the sphincter muscles of bladder or anus. Just as the infant discovered a pleasure gain as a by-product of food intake via the mouth, he now experiences a pleasure gain as a by-product of his excretory activities. The area around his anus becomes at this time the most important body zone. Just as in the suckling period the child obtained mouth-pleasure by finger sucking independent of food intake, so he now tries by withholding his feces and playing with that part of his body to obtain pleasure from his anal region. If toilet training actively prevents him from doing this, he succeeds in at least preserving the memory of such pleasures by engaging in the more acceptable games with sand, water, mud, and much later in his "smearing" with paints.

Adults have always complained that at this period children are dirty and messy. But they were also always inclined to excuse the child as being still small and stupid, with his aesthetic sense not yet sufficiently developed to understand the difference between clean and dirty, or his sense of smell not exercised enough to distinguish between sweet and offensive.

I am of the opinion that the observers of children were prejudiced here and committed an error of judgment.

Whoever observes a small child at approximately age 2 will notice that there is nothing wrong with his sense of smell. He merely differs from adults in his appraisal of the various smells. The scent of a flower which delights an adult will leave the child quite indifferent unless he has over a period of time been taught to say, "Oh, how lovely!" when smelling a flower. However, what smells horrid to us smells good to the child, an attitude which adults consider as blameworthy.

Other characteristics of children fall into the same category. For centuries people have remarked on the cruelty of children, blaming it on their lack of understanding. When a child tears off the legs and wings of butterflies and insects, kills or tortures birds, or vents his destructive urges on toys or articles in daily use, his elders have generally excused this on the ground of his lacking empathy with different living creatures, or his lacking comprehension for the money value of things.

But in this respect, too, our observation teaches us something different. We believe that the child tortures animals, not because he does not understand that he is inflicting pain, but precisely because he wants to inflict pain, and for this purpose small, defenseless beetles are the most suitable and least dangerous of creatures. The child destroys objects because the actual value of such things is negligible, compared with the joy he experiences in their destruction. Again we can guess the motive for this behavior from the expression of his face and the intense joy with which he pursues his purpose. He behaves as he does because it gives him pleasure.

After toilet training has attained its aim, and the child, in spite of his opposition, has been taught how to control his movements, the anal zone loses its role for the provision of pleasurable sensations. Its place is taken by an even more important part of the body. The child begins to play with his genitals. At this time his thirst for knowledge is directed toward the discovery of the differences between the sexes.

He delights in showing his sexual parts naked to other children, and in return demands to see theirs. His passion for asking questions, of which his elders complain, has as its basis these problems—the difference between the sexes and its connection with the origin of children, which he somehow or other dimly feels. Unfortunately, the high point of development which in several respects is reached by the child at this time, i.e., age 4 or 5, appears to the adults also as the high point of objectionable habits.

Throughout the whole period of time described above, the child behaves as if nothing were more important than the pursuit of his own pleasures and the gratification of his powerful instinctual wishes, whereas the adults act as if the prevention of these aims was their most important task. What results from this is a never-ending battle between child and adults. The latter want to replace the child's pleasure in dirt by disgust for it, shamelessness by shame, cruelty by pity, destructiveness by care. Curiosity about the body and play with body parts should be eliminated by prohibitions, lack of consideration for others changed into considerateness, and egoism converted into altruism. Step by step education aims at the exact opposite of what the child wants, and at each step it regards as desirable the very opposite of the child's inherent instinctual strivings.

As we have seen, to the child the attainment of pleasure is the main object of life. The adult wants to teach him to regard the claims of the external world as more important than internal urges. The child is impatient, he cannot endure any delay and acts only for what concerns him at the moment; the adult teaches him to postpone the gratification of impulses and to think of the future.

It will have struck you that in my description there is no

essential distinction made between the pleasure gained from finger sucking and from playing with the genitals, i.e., masturbation. As a matter of fact, from the standpoint of psychoanalysis no such distinction exists. All the pleasurable acts described here strive for the satisfaction of instinctual impulses. Psychoanalysis invests them all with sexual significance, whether they are carried out directly on the sexual organs, or the mouth, or the anus. The role which the genitals play in the fourth or fifth year of the child's life is identical with that of the mouth in the first year or the anus in the second year. The genital zone appears to us as so significant only in retrospect when we regard it from the standpoint of the adult's sex life, where the genitals are the executive organs of sex. But even then the pleasure-yielding zones of early childhood retain a certain significance. The sensual pleasure derived from them serves as a preparation for and an introduction to the sexual act proper.

The fact that the bodily areas from which the young child gains his first sensual pleasures play a part, though a subordinate one, in the sexual life of the adult may not seem to you to be sufficient reason for designating these areas and the child's pleasure-seeking activities at them as sexual. But psychoanalysis justifies this classification on account of still another circumstance. There are abnormal cases in which the gratification of one or another of these infantile impulses never becomes subordinated to that obtained at the genital zone, but retains primacy and dominates the adult's sexual life to the exclusion of normal sex. Such persons are called perverts. It is characteristic of them that in a very important aspect of their life, namely, in their sexuality, they have remained at the stage of the little child, or possibly, at some time or another, have returned to that stage.

The understanding of this abnormality in adult sexual life offers a first explanation why the adult world is so very zealous in restraining the child from the gratification of his impulses. The phases of development through which the child has to pass should be no more than stations on the way to a prescribed goal. When one of these stopping places appears too attractive to the child, there is the danger that he will want to settle down there permanently and refuse to continue the journey, i.e., to advance to a further stage of development. Long before there was any scientific evidence for this conception, those in charge of children have acted as if they recognized these dangers and regarded it as their task to drive the child through his phases of development without his ever attaining any real satisfaction and pleasure from any one stage except the last.

The means which from time immemorial were adopted to prevent the child from obtaining these dreaded gratifications are of two kinds. The child may be warned: if you continue to suck your thumb, it will be cut off, a threat repeated on many occasions and with every kind of variation. It is meant to frighten the child by the idea of actual injury to a necessary and much-prized part of his body, and thereby induce him to renounce the pleasure gained from it. Or parents may say: if you do that I cannot love you anymore, facing the child with the possibility of losing his parents' love. Both threats derive their effectiveness from the child's situation as we have already learned to understand it, i.e., his complete helplessness and powerlessness in the midst of an overwhelming adult world, and his exclusive dependence upon his parents' care for him.

Both methods are usually equally effective. Under the pressure of such appalling dangers the child, indeed, learns to abandon his primitive wishes. At first he merely pretends to have changed his attitude, either because he fears or because he loves the adult. He begins to call horrid what seems nice to him, and to consider as good what he dislikes. As he identifies increasingly with the adults, he also accepts their values as the true ones. He even begins to forget that he has ever felt otherwise. Gradually he turns away from everything he had desired in his earlier days, and blocks a return to his earlier pleasures by an absolute reversal of the feelings connected with the former satisfactions. The more completely he succeeds in this transformation, the more contented are the grownups with the result of their efforts.

This renunciation of the pleasures derived from his infantile impulses has two important consequences for the individual's mental development. He applies the standards which have been enforced on him to the rest of the world and becomes intolerant toward those who have not achieved the same. The moral indignation which is aroused in him by any such acts of indulgence is the measure of the effort he himself has had to make to conquer his infantile instinctual impulses.

But as his memory turns away from the pleasurable experiences once so highly prized, all the feelings and experiences which belong to this whole period of life are simultaneously pushed out. He forgets his past, which now in retrospect can appear to him only as unworthy and repulsive. And thereby, precisely, he acquires that gap in his memory, that impenetrable barrier, and that inaccessibility with regard to the first most important experiences of childhood which appeared so surprising when we met this fact in the last lecture.

3

The Latency Period

During the two previous lectures I have kept you far removed from the sphere of your own particular interests. I have engaged your attention for the emotional condition and the development of the instinctual drives of the tiny child—a subject, indeed, which you probably believe to have practical significance only for mothers, nurses, or, at the most, for nursery school teachers. I should not like you to think, on account of my choice of material, that I underestimate the problems which arise in your work with older children. But my object was to bring before you in the course of these lectures many of the fundamental ideas of psychoanalysis, and, in order to develop them vividly for you, I required some very definite material which only the first years of childhood can supply.

To justify the roundabout way I have led you, let us examine what you have learned from it. I began with the psychoanalytic assertion that human beings are acquainted with only a fragment of their own inner life, and know nothing about a great many of the feelings and thoughts which go on within them—that is to say, that these happen *unconsciously*, without their awareness. You may have been tempted to reply that one must not expect too much from the power of memory. In view of the vast mass of stimuli pressing upon man from within and without, it is surely not possible to retain everything in consciousness; it should suffice if one knows the most important things about oneself. But then the example of the big gap in memory concerning the childhood years contradicted this assumption. I was able to show you that the importance of an event is by no means a guarantee for its persistence in our memory; indeed, on the contrary, there are highly significant impressions which only too often escape recollection. Added to this was the fact that this submerged part of the inner world has the curious characteristic of retaining its dynamic force when it disappears from memory. It exercises a decisive influence on the child's life, shapes his relations to the people around him, and reveals itself in his daily behavior. This double aspect of childhood experiences—their disappearance into a void while retaining the power to exert influence—has served as an illustration of the concept of the *unconscious* in psychoanalysis.

You have also learned what brings about the forgetting of important impressions. The child himself might be inclined to retain fond memories of his first very highly valued wishes and their satisfaction if he were not subjected to external pressure. It is due to this that he turns away from them, pushes them aside with a great expenditure of energy, and finally no longer wants to know anything about them. We say, then, that he has *repressed* them.

You have further heard that even when the child has achieved this act of repression, those who educate him are not yet satisfied with this accomplishment. There is always the danger that what has been pushed aside might at an opportune moment return from the depths. Therefore every obstacle is put in the way of its reemergence. As described above, this leads to the reversal of the child's original feelings and character traits. Let us assume, for example, that a child of about 2 years feels the urge to put his excreta into his mouth. Under the impact of education he learns not only to reject what he now has come to know as dirty and thus to renounce his original wish, but also to feel disgusted by it. This means that contact with excrement now makes him feel nauseous, the wish to vomit taking the place of the original wish to put something into his mouth. To use his mouth for such a purpose has become impossible for him owing to disgust. Psychoanalysis calls such an attribute, acquired in a conflict with and as a reaction to an infantile impulse, a *reaction formation*. When later on we discover in an older child an unusually strong feeling of pity, a heightened sense of shame, or especially easily aroused reactions of disgust, we may conclude that in his earliest years he had been especially cruel, shameless, or dirty. It is essential for these reaction formations to be strong so that they can prevent relapses into those earlier habits.

However, this turn to the exact opposite in the form of a reaction formation is only one of the ways in which the child can discard unwanted attributes. Another way already mentioned is to transform an undesirable activity into a

more desirable one. The little child who has enjoyed playing about with his excreta need not completely forego this
pleasure in order to escape the condemnation of those who
bring him up. He can turn to a related pleasure, for example, by substituting play with sand and water for play with
feces and urine. According to the opportunities given him,
he can then build things in a sandbox, dig in the garden, or,
in the case of little girls, enjoy washing dolls' clothes. The
pleasure in smearing can, as already indicated, continue as
pleasure in painting and coloring. In each of these socially
approved and often useful activities, the child enjoys some
portion of the pleasure originally experienced. To this re-
finement of an impulse, and its deflection to a more highly
valued aim, psychoanalysis has given the name of *sublimation.*

You have, however, been able to gather from the two previous lectures something more than merely the definition
of some of the basic concepts of psychoanalysis. You have
learned that certain images and ideas become definitely
linked together in the child's mind, and that these idea-
tional patterns or complexes play an outstanding role in
his emotional life. They dominate certain years of his life,
before they are repressed and disappear from the consciousness of the adult. An example of such an association of
ideas is the relationship of the little child to his parents.
Psychoanalysis, as you have already heard, discovers behind
this the same motives and desires which inspired the deeds
of King Oedipus, and has given the name of the *Oedipus
complex* to it. Another such complex of ideas is due to the
effect of the threats employed to make the child submit to
the adults' wishes. As it is the purport of these threats, however vague, to cut off an important part of the child's body

—his hand, or tongue, or penis—psychoanalysis has named this complex the *castration complex*.

Furthermore, you became acquainted with the fact that the way in which a child experiences these earliest complexes, especially his relations with his parents, becomes the prototype for all later experience. There is in the individual a compulsion to repeat in later life the pattern of his earlier love and hate, rebellion and submission, disloyalty and loyalty. It is not a matter of indifference for the child's future that there is an inner urge to choose love relations, friends, and even the professional career in a way which enables an almost unchanged reedition of the repressed childhood events. We say, as given in the example of the pupil-teacher relationship, that the child *transfers* his emotional attitudes from a figure in his past onto a person in the present. It is obvious that this cannot happen without a variety of misunderstandings and distortions of the present situation.

Finally, you found in my description of the child's instinctual development a confirmation of the often-heard assertion that psychoanalysis extends the concept of sexuality beyond the hitherto customary limits. It designates as sexual a series of childish activities which had formerly been regarded as harmless and far removed from anything sexual. In contrast to other beliefs known to you, psychoanalysis asserts that human sexuality does not suddenly come into being between the thirteenth and fifteenth year, i.e., at puberty, but operates from the outset of the child's development, changes gradually from one form to another, progresses from stage to stage, until at last adult sexual life is achieved as the final result of a long sequence. The energy with which the sexual drive functions in all these phases is qualitatively always the same, though it differs in quantity at different periods. Psychoanalysis calls this sexual energy *libido*. While the theory of the child's instinctual development is the most important part of the new psychoanalytic discipline, it is also the reason for most of its unpopularity. Very likely this is also the explanation why many of you have until now stayed away from analytic teachings.

I think you may be content with this summary of knowledge so far acquired. You have become acquainted with some of the most important psychoanalytic terms and concepts: the unconscious, repression, reaction formation, sublimation, transference, the Oedipus complex and the castration complex, the libido and the theory of infantile sexuality. These new concepts will most likely help us very much in our further task, that of investigating the next period in the child's life.

We continue our description of the child's development from the point where we left off. This was at age 5 or 6, at the time when the child enters school and consequently claims all your interest.

In the light of what we know by now, let us examine again the teachers' complaints that the children are already finished human beings when they arrive. We can now confirm the accuracy of this impression. By the time he enters nursery school or school, the child has already passed through a host of profound emotional experiences. He has suffered a curtailment of his original egoism through love for the parents; he has experienced a violent desire for the possession of the beloved mother; and he has defended his rights by death wishes directed against others and by outbreaks of jealousy. In relation to the father he has developed feelings of respect and admiration, tormenting feelings of competition with a stronger rival, the sense of impotence, and the depressing impact of a disappointment in love. He has, moreover, already passed through a complicated instinctual development and has learned how hard it is to be compelled to repudiate a part of one's own personality. Under the pressure of education he has suffered strong fears and anxiety, and accomplished enormous changes within himself. Burdened with this past, the child is indeed anything but a blank sheet.

The transformation which has taken place within him is truly amazing. The animallike creature, so dependent on others, and almost unbearable in his behavior has evolved into a more or less reasonable human being. The schoolchild who enters the classroom is prepared to find that there he is only one among many, and cannot count on any privileged position. He has learned something of social adaptation. Instead of constantly seeking to gratify his desires, as he did formerly, he is now prepared to do what is required of him and to confine his pleasures to the times allotted for this purpose. His interest in uncovering the intimate secrets of his environment has now been transformed into a thirst for knowledge and a love of learning. In place of the revelations and explanations which he longed for earlier he is now willing to obtain knowledge of letters and numbers.

The day care workers among you may think that I am describing the good behavior of the child in too glowing colors, just as in my last talk with you I painted his misbehaviors too black. You feel that none of the children you know are as good as that. But let us not forget that the day centers, as they operate today, receive only those whose early upbringing has failed, whether for internal or external reasons. In contrast, those who teach in ordinary schools may recognize many of their pupils in my description and will not accuse me of exaggeration.

So far as my description is correct, it is indeed a splendid proof of the practical possibilities and the enormous influence of education. The parents to whom, speaking generally, we ascribe the credit for the earliest education of the child have every right to be proud if they have succeeded in turning the crying, troublesome, and dirty infant into a well-behaved schoolchild. There are not many areas anywhere where similar transformations are accomplished.

However, we should admire the work which the parents have performed more unreservedly if in judging its results two considerations were not forced upon us. One of these arises from observation. Whoever has had the opportunity of dealing with children of 3 or 4 is amazed at the wealth of their fantasy, the extent of their perceptiveness, the lucidity of their minds, and the inflexible logic of their questions and conclusions. Yet the very same children, when they reach school age, appear to the adult rather mediocre and commonplace. We ask with astonishment whatever has become of the child's cleverness and originality.

Psychoanalysis reveals to us that these gifts of the very young have not been able to withstand the demands which have been made upon him; after the expiration of his fifth year they are as good as gone. Evidently, to raise children to be "good" is not without its dangers. The repressions which are required to achieve this result, the reaction formations and the sublimations which have been built up, are paid for at the price of originality and spontaneity. Thus, if the older children, compared with the younger ones, strike us as duller and more inactive, the impression is absolutely correct. The limitations which are placed upon their thinking, and the obstacles put in the way of their primitive activities, result in restrictions of thinking and inhibitions of acting.

While, thus, parents need not be too proud of their success, in another respect as well it is somewhat doubtful how much credit they deserve. We seem to have no guarantee at all whether the good behavior of the older child is the product of education or simply the consequence of having reached a certain stage of development. So far we have no evidence to help us decide what would happen if young children were allowed to develop without interference. We do not know whether they would grow up like little savages or whether, without any external help, they would spontaneously pass through a series of successive modifications. It is quite certain that education influences the child tremendously in various directions, but the question remains unanswered what would happen if the adults around a child refrained from checking him in any way.

One important psychoanalytic experiment concerning this question was made, but unfortunately not completed. In 1921, the Russian analyst, Vera Schmidt, founded in Moscow a residential home for thirty children aged 1 to 5 years. The name she gave to it, Children's Home Laboratory, stressed its character as a scientific experiment. Vera Schmidt's plan was to surround this small group of children with scientifically trained teachers employed to observe quietly their various emotional and instinctual manifestations; and though the teachers would help and stimulate, they were to interfere as little as possible with the changes that were taking place in the children's personalities. By such means it would gradually be established whether the various phases which follow one another in the child's first years arise spontaneously and disappear again without any direct educational influence, and also whether the child, without being forced, would abandon his pleasurable activities and their sources after a certain period and exchange them for new ones.

On account of external difficulties, Vera Schmidt's Children's Home Laboratory was not maintained long enough to complete the experiment, except for the case of one child. How much credit for the changes in the child is to be ascribed exclusively to the earliest education remains, therefore, an unsolved question until it becomes possible perhaps to undertake similar experiments under more favorable circumstances.

But whatever the answer, observation in any case teaches us that in the fifth or sixth year the overwhelming force of the infantile drives dies down slowly. The high point in the violent emotional manifestations and insistent instinctual wishes has passed and the child gradually quiets down. It appears as if he had taken a great leap to become all at once fully adult, just as the animal develops from birth to sexual maturity without a break, and does not change further afterward. But with human beings, the course of development is different. Approximately at age 5 drive development comes to a standstill without having reached a final point. Interest in the gratification of his drives declines and the child really begins to resemble the image of the "good" child which had previously existed only in the wishful imagination of his elders.

Nevertheless, his instinctual urges have not ceased to exist; they have merely disappeared from the surface. They are latent, dormant, and wake up again with renewed vigor

after a period of time. Puberty, which has so long been regarded as the age when sexual drives have their beginning,
is thus merely a second edition of a development which began at birth, came to a standstill at the end of the first
period of childhood, and now is indeed finally completed.

If we follow the growth of a child from the earliest time,
through the quiet phase—called, in psychoanalysis, the
latency period—to puberty, we find that all the old problems, after being dormant, reemerge. Conflicts such as
rivalry with the father, forbidden pleasures such as love of
dirt, will reappear and create great difficulties. Thus the earliest period of the child's life often shows far-reaching similarities with the period of adolescence. And yet in the
calmer latency period the child resembles in many respects
a sensible settled adult.

Here again, from time immemorial, education has acted
as if it had been guided by a good psychological understanding of the child's inner situation. It utilizes the
latency period, when the child is less disturbed by his drives
and not exclusively engrossed in his inner conflicts, to begin
the training of his intellect. Schoolteachers have always behaved as if they understood that the child is the more
capable of learning the less subject he is to his instinctual
urges, and consequently they have disapproved of and
punished any schoolchild who seeks drive gratification.

Here the tasks of school and day care diverge. The object
of the school is above all else instruction—i.e., the development of the intellect, the imparting of new knowledge, and
the stimulation of mental capacities. Day care services, in
contrast, have the task of belatedly making up for failures
in the child's training to curb his drive activity. Day care
workers know they have only a limited time at their dis-

posal; they know that puberty in which the sexual instinct bursts forth anew and overwhelms the child with its force also marks the end for their educational efforts. But the success or failure of this aftereducation may in many cases determine whether at this last opportunity it was still possible to establish a reasonable harmony between the child's ego, the urgency of his impulses, and the demands of society.

You may also wish to know how the possibilities of education in infancy and in the latency period are related to one another. Is there a difference between the attitude of the young child to his parents and that of the older child to his teachers and tutors? Does the teacher simply inherit the role of the parents, and must he play the part of the parents, and, as they do, work with threats of castration, fear of loss of love, and expressions of tenderness? When we think of the difficulties which the child has to endure at the height of his Oedipus complex, we are right to be alarmed at the idea of similar conflicts, multiplied by numbers, to be suffered in the contact between a group of children and its teacher. How can a professional worker play the part of mother or father successfully in a large day care center, and do justice to the claims of each individual child without arousing outbreaks of jealousy on all sides? Or how can the teacher remain continually the object of fear, the target of insurgent tendencies, and yet at the same time be the personal friend of each individual child?

What we must not forget is that the child's emotional situation has changed in the meantime; his relations to his parents no longer assume the old form. As the infantile drives begin to weaken in the latency period, the passionate feelings which have hitherto dominated the relation of the child to his parents are mitigated. Again we do not know whether this change simply corresponds to the new phase of development, or whether the child's passionate love demands gradually succumb to many unavoidable disappointments and frustrations.

In any case, the relationship between child and parents becomes calmer, less passionate, and less exclusive. The child begins to see his parents in a more reasonable light and to correct his overestimation of his father, whom until now he has regarded as omnipotent. Love of the mother which at the height of the early infantile period resembled adult love in the intensity of its passion and insatiableness gives way to a tenderness which makes fewer claims and is no longer devoid of criticism. At the same time the child tries to obtain a certain amount of freedom from his parents, and begins to seek additional objects for his love and admiration. He initiates a process of detachment which continues throughout the whole of the latency period. It is a sign of satisfactory development if, at the termination of puberty, the dependence on the love objects of childhood comes to an end. The sexual drive, having passed successfully through all the intervening phases, then reaches the adult genital stage, and should attach itself to a love object outside the individual's own family.

However, the child's detachment from his earliest and most important love objects succeeds only on one very definite condition. It is as if the parents said: you can certainly go away, but you must take us with you. This means that the influence of the parents does not end with removal from them and not even with the abatement of feeling for them. Their influence simply changes from an external to an internal one. We know that the young child obeys his parents' orders only when they are actually present, i.e., when he has to fear a direct reprimand or their personal interference. Left alone, he follows his own wishes without scruple. This behavior changes after age 2 or 3. Even when the person in authority has left the room, he will know then what is permitted and what is forbidden, and he will behave accordingly. We say that besides the forces that influence him from outside he has also developed an inner force—an inner voice—which determines his actions.

Among psychoanalysts there exists no doubt about the origin of this inner voice, the conscience, as it is generally called. It is the continuation of the voice of the parents which is now operative from within instead of, as formerly, from without. The child has absorbed, as it were, a part of his father or mother, or rather the commands and prohibitions which he has constantly received from them, and has made them an essential part of his being. In the course of growing up this internalized parental part assumes increasingly the demanding and forbidding role of the parents in the external world and continues from within the education of the child, even without the parent's backing. The child accords to this internalized authority a special place of honor in his own ego, regards it as an ideal, and is prepared to submit to it, often more slavishly than in his younger days he had submitted to his actual parents.

The poor ego of the child must from now on throughout his life strive to fulfill the demands of this ideal—the *superego*, as psychoanalysis names it. When the child disobeys it, he feels an inner dissatisfaction or guilt. When he acts in accordance with the superego, he feels pleased with himself, self-satisfied. Thus the old relations between child and parents are perpetuated within the child, and the severity or mildness with which the parents have treated the child is reflected to a degree in the attitude of superego to ego.

Returning to an earlier statement, we can now say: the price which the child has to pay for detaching himself from his parents is their incorporation in his own personality. The success of this incorporation is at the same time also the measure of the permanency of what education has accomplished.

Our former question concerning the differences between education in early childhood and in the latency period is now no longer difficult to answer.

The earliest educators and the small child are opposed to each other like two factions. The parents want something that the child does not want; the child wants what the parents do not want. The child pursues his aims with undivided passion; all the parents can do is to resort to bribes, threats, or forcible measures. Here one goal is diametrically opposed to the other. The fact that the victory is usually won by the parents is to be ascribed only to their superior power.

In the latency period the situation is altogether different. The child that now confronts the adult is no longer an undivided being. He is, as we have learned, divided within himself. Even if his ego occasionally still pursues its earlier aims, his superego, the successor to his parents, is on the side of the educators. The extent of the educational possibilities is now determined by the intelligence of the adults. They are misguided if they persist in treating the child in the latency period as though that child were still in absolute opposition; by so doing they deprive themselves of a great advantage. What they ought to do is to recognize the split within the child and to act accordingly. If they succeed in allying themselves with the child's superego, the battle for drive control and social adaptation will be won.

Our question regarding the relations between the teacher and the class or group also is now easier to answer. We see from the above that the teacher inherits more than merely the child's Oedipus complex. He assumes for each of the children under his control the role of superego, and in this way acquires the right to their submission. If he merely represented a parent for each child, then all the unsolved conflicts of early childhood would be enacted around him; moreover, his group would be torn asunder by rivalry and jealousies. But if he does succeed in representing their superego, the ideal of the group, the compulsory obedience changes into voluntary submission. Moreover, all the children under his guidance will develop ties to each other and become a united group.

4

The Relation Between Psychoanalysis and Education

We must not demand too much from one another. You must not expect that in four short lectures I shall succeed in presenting to you more than the most important principles of a discipline the study of which requires as many years. I, on the other hand, cannot expect you to remember all the details which I have put before you. My survey of the relevant subjects was highly condensed and probably often confusing. You may not be able to retain more than at best three of the characteristic viewpoints of psychoanalysis as guidelines for your work.

The first of these viewpoints is concerned with chronology. Psychoanalysis distinguishes, as you have heard, three different periods in the life of the child: early childhood up to about the end of the fifth year; the latency period to the beginning of preadolescence about the eleventh, twelfth, or thirteenth year; and adolescence itself, which leads into adult life. Each of these periods is characterized by different emotional reactions of the child to the adult world and by a different stage of drive development. A specific attribute or behavior of the child cannot therefore be judged without reference to the specific period of his life.

Acts of cruelty or shamelessness, for example, which in early childhood and in adolescence are normal, will appear ominous if observed in the latency period, and, in adult life, may have to be assessed as perverse. The strong tie to the parents, which is natural and desirable in the first years and in the latency period, is a sign of retarded development if it still persists at the end of adolescence. The strong urge to rebel against authority, which in adolescence facilitates entry into normal adult life, may be an obstacle to ego development in early childhood or in the latency period.

The second viewpoint concerns the internal structuring of the child's personality. Until now you may have pictured the children with whom you are dealing as homogeneous beings, and consequently have been puzzled by the contradictions in their behavior, the difference between what they want to do and what they are able to do, the discrepancy between their intentions and their actions. Psychoanalysis shows you the personality of the child to be divided into three parts: his instinctual life, his reasonable ego, and his superego, which is derived from the relationship with his parents. The contradictions in the child's behavior will become understandable, therefore, when you learn to see the different reactions as expressions of that particular part of his being which at the particular moment predominates. The third viewpoint is concerned with the interactions between these agencies within the child. Far from being in a quiescent state, these behave as forces struggling with each other. When, for example, the ego opposes an instinctual wish which the child knows to be undesirable, the outcome of the conflict depends upon the relative strength of the libido at the disposal of the wish compared with the energy of the repressing force instigated by the superego.

But I fear that even these three simplified and practically applicable principles do not yet give you all that you hoped to get from psychoanalysis. Probably you seek practical advice rather than an extension of theoretical knowledge. You surely want to know which tools of education are most to be recommended; which have to be absolutely avoided if you do not want to imperil the child's whole development. Above all, you want to know whether we, as adults, should interfere more or be less authoritarian than adults have been in the past.

In answer to the last question I have to say that psychoanalysis so far has stood for limiting the efforts of education by emphasizing some specific dangers connected with it. I remind you in this respect of the manner in which the child comes to fulfill the demands of the adult world; how he overcomes his first strong emotional attachments by identification with the beloved and feared adults; how he escapes from their external influence, but meanwhile erects an agency within himself, which, modeled on their authority, continues to maintain their influence. It is this incorporation of the parent figure which is a dangerous step, since due to it the parents' prohibitions and demands become fixed and unchangeable, i.e., historical residues which are incapable of adapting themselves to external changes. Naturally, the parents themselves have been prepared to see the 30-year-old man do what they forbade the 3-year-old child. But that part of a person's ego which is a precipitate of their demands and standards is not open to such changes; it remains inexorable.

I give, in what follows, some examples to elucidate these points. I am thinking of a boy who was extremely fond of sweets in his early years. As this passion was too great to be satisfied by legitimate means, he hit upon all kinds of forbidden plans and dodges in order to get hold of what he wanted, spent all his pocket money on sweets, and was not too particular about how he procured additional funds. Here, the adults intervened. The boy was forbidden sweets, and his devotion to the mother who stood for the prohibition gave special emphasis to it. The craving disappeared, to the satisfaction of his elders. Yet even later, this lad, then a young man with plenty of money who could easily buy up all the cakes of the confectionery shops, was not able to eat a piece of chocolate without blushing furiously. Whoever observed him could only feel convinced that he was doing something forbidden—such as eating what is bought with stolen money. Obviously, the restriction imposed upon him earlier did not automatically yield to the changed situation.

Listen to another example, this time even less harmless. It concerns a boy specially devoted to his mother. What he wished above all was to replace his father, to be her confidant, protector, and best-beloved. Repeatedly, he had to experience that his father was the rightful owner of the position for which he was striving; that the father had the power to send him away from his mother whenever he wanted, thereby impressing upon him the difference between his own childish helplessness and impotence and his father's overwhelming strength. Later, as an adolescent, this boy showed a tormenting timidity and insecurity whenever he found himself in the same house with a girl he admired. The content of his fear was that somebody might appear and declare that he was sitting or standing in a place which belonged to somebody else. To avoid this extremely embarrassing situation a great deal of his energy was employed in preparing excuses which could plausibly explain his presence.

Or take another case. A small girl developed an excessive pleasure in her naked body, showed herself naked to her brothers and sisters, and delighted in running through the rooms stark naked before going to bed. Education stepped in and the child made a great effort to suppress her desire. This resulted in intense feelings of shame and modesty which continued in later life. When the question of choosing a career arose, somebody suggested an occupation which would necessitate her sharing a room with companions. Unhesitatingly she stated that this was not for her. Behind the apparently rational motivation she ultimately revealed the fear of undressing in the presence of others. What profession to choose was less important than the prohibition carried over from childhood.

The psychoanalyst whose therapeutic work consists of resolving such inhibitions and developmental disturbances cannot help but see education from its worst aspect. Here, he feels, the adults have truly been overdoing it! Would it not have been better to have placed somewhat less emphasis on decorum and convention, to have permitted child number one to be greedy, child number two to imagine himself in the role of the father, the third child to run about naked, and a fourth perhaps to play with his genitals? Would these childish gratifications really have had any effect as adverse as the damage wrought by their prohibition? What education has done is to split the child's personality; to incite internal conflicts; to diminish the child's capacity to love freely; to render him incapable of enjoyment and inhibited in work. The analyst to whom all this is apparent resolves, so far as he is concerned, not to participate in such efforts, but to leave his own children free rather than to educate them in this way. He decides to risk their being somewhat unruly rather than enforcing on them such crippling of their personalities.

But now, I feel sure, that you are shocked by the one-sidedness of my views. It is high time to change the viewpoint. Education appears to us in a very different light when viewed not from the aspect of neurotic inhibition but, for example, from the aspect of delinquency, as August Aichhorn has done in his book on *Wayward Youth* (1925).

The neglected or wayward child, says Aichhorn, refuses to take his place in society. He does not succeed sufficiently in inhibiting drive gratification; he cannot divert enough energy from his sexual drives to employ it for purposes more highly valued by society. He refuses, therefore, to submit to the restrictions which are binding for the community in which he lives, and withdraws from any participation in its life and work. No one who has had to deal with these youngsters either educationally or therapeutically can fail to regret that with them education did not succeed in first imposing external checks to be transformed later into internal standards.

Take as an example a child who for some time occupied the attention of the Vienna Children's Court. This 8-year-old girl was equally impossible in her behavior at home and at school. From every residential home she was invariably returned to her parents, after a few days. She refused to learn anything or to share in the activities of other children. She pretended to be stupid, and did this so efficiently that in several places she was diagnosed as mentally defective. In the classroom she lay down on a bench and masturbated, reacting to any interference with shrieks of anger. At home she was ill-treated since this was the only way the parents could think of dealing with her. An analytic investigation showed two things. The external circumstances were peculiarly unfavorable to the development of any kind of emotional relations between the child and her environment. No one offered the love which would in some way have compensated the child for giving up the gratification obtained from her own body; nor did the severe punishments from which the parents expected a restraining influence fulfill this purpose. The girl had developed such strong masochistic tendencies that each beating merely became another stimulus for sexual excitement and activity. Compare this case of neglect with the one of inhibition described above. This child also did not become a free and self-reliant human being, but merely a cowed creature whose moral development had stopped simultaneously with her mental growth.

In his book *Wayward Youth* Aichhorn mentioned another severe case of maldevelopment—that of a boy who from about his sixth year onward had been offered every kind of sexual gratification by his mother, and finally, after reaching sexual maturity, had regular sexual intercourse with her. He had thus actually experienced what other children wish for in their fantasy. But this boy, too, with all restrictions removed, by no means developed into a self-reliant harmonious, vigorous human being.

What had occurred in his development was a kind of "short-circuiting." By the actual fulfillment of his childhood wishes he was saved the necessity of traversing the whole laborious path toward adulthood. He did not need to become a grown man in order to attain all the possibilities of gratification permitted to a man. But whatever he had escaped, he paid for by giving up all further development.

However, you may think that the problem is not quite as difficult as I have represented it to you. Neurotic inhibition and delinquency may be merely extreme results, showing on the one hand the injurious effect of excessive interference, and on the other hand the harm done by the lack of all restraints. The task of upbringing based on analytic understanding is to find a middle road between these extremes —that is to say, to find for each stage in the child's life the right proportion between drive gratification and drive control.

Possibly a detailed description of this new analytic type of education should have been the content of my lectures. But for this it is too early. What we have so far is only a small group of adults, teachers and parents, who have been analyzed themselves, and now seek to apply to the upbringing of children the understanding that psychoanalysis has brought to their own life. It may be some time still before enough is known and enough has been tried out so that the application of analytic principles can be demonstrated for general use.

Nevertheless, it would be wrong to conclude that psychoanalysis has nothing to offer you now except hopes for the future; and that it is not yet profitable for teachers engaged in practical work to study psychoanalysis. There is no need to wait and see whether psychoanalysis can do anything for education.

I maintain that even today psychoanalysis does three things for it. In the first place, it is well qualified to offer criticism of existing methods. In the second place, as a scientific theory of the instinctual drives, the unconscious, and the libido, psychoanalysis extends the educator's knowledge of the complicated relations between child and adults. Finally, as a method of therapy, the analysis of children endeavors to repair the injuries which have been inflicted upon the child during the process of education.

The following example illustrates the second point, i.e., the elucidation of the situation between child and adult by insight into the unconscious background of conscious behavior.

An excellent woman teacher began her career in her eighteenth year when, in consequence of unhappy family circumstances, she left home to take a position as governess to three boys. The second boy presented a serious educational problem. He was backward in his lessons and appeared very timid, reserved, and dull; he played a subordinate role in the family, with his parents constantly favoring and preferring his two gifted and attractive brothers. The governess devoted all her efforts and interest to the middle boy, and in a comparatively short time had obtained a wonderful success.

The boy grew very fond of her, was more devoted to her than he had ever been to anybody before, and became frank and friendly in his ways. His interest in learning increased, and she succeeded in teaching him in one year the subjects laid down for two years, so that he was no longer behind in his work. The parents were now proud of this child, whom until then they had treated with but slight affection; they took much more trouble about him; and his relations to them and also to his brothers improved, until he was finally accepted as a most valued member of the family circle.

But thereupon an unexpected difficulty arose. The governess to whom the success was due now began on her side to have trouble with the boy so that she withdrew her love from him. Finally, she left the house, where she was greatly appreciated, on account of the very child who in the beginning had exerted the strongest attraction on her.

The psychoanalysis which she underwent nearly fifteen years later revealed to her the true facts of the case. In her own family, as a child, she had, with more or less justification, imagined herself to be the unloved child—the same position in which she had actually found the boy when she began her work with him. On the basis of this similar fate she had seen herself in this boy, and had identified herself with him. All the love and care which she had lavished upon him meant that she was really saying to herself: "That is the way I ought to have been treated to make something of me." Success, when it came, destroyed this identification. It turned her charge into a being who could no longer be identified with her own life. The hostile feelings toward him arose from envy; she could not help begrudging him the success which she herself had never attained.

You will say, perhaps, that it was a good thing that this governess, when dealing with her pupil, had not yet been analyzed; otherwise we should have lost a fine educational success. But I feel that these educational successes are too dearly bought. They are paid for by the failures with those children who are not fortunate enough to display symptoms or suffering which remind their teachers of their own childhood, and for this reason arouse empathy. I hold we are justified in demanding that teachers should have learned to know and to control their own conflicts before they begin educational work. Otherwise the children merely serve as more or less suitable material on which to abreact unconscious and unsolved difficulties.

But even in assessing children, we need analytic help to understand their manifest behavior. The following notes which a boy dictated as the opening of a book he planned to write are an example of this. He called the fragment:

THE WRONG THINGS GROWN-PEOPLE DO

Here, you grown-up people, listen to me, if you want to know something! Don't be too cocky because children can't do everything that grown-up people do. But they can do most of what you do. But children will never obey if you order them about like this, for example: "Now go and undress, quickly, get going." Then they will never undress, don't you believe it. But when you speak nicely, then they will do it at once. You think you can do whatever you want to do, but don't imagine any such thing. And don't constantly say: "You must do this, you *must* do that!" No one *must* do things, neither therefore *must* children do things. You think children *must* wash themselves. Certainly not. Then you say, "But if you don't wash, everybody will say, 'Oh fie, how dirty he is!' and so you *must* wash yourself." No, he mustn't, but he does wash, so that people won't call him dirty.

When you tell children what they are to do that's enough, and don't tell them so much about how they are to do it, for they do what they think right, just as you do. And don't always say to them, "You mustn't buy such and such a thing," for if they pay for it themselves they can buy what they like. Don't always say to children, "You can't do that!" For they can do many things better than you, and you won't ever believe it, and afterward you are astonished. Don't always talk so much; let the children sometimes get a word in!

Now, suppose that these notes were found in a school and taken to the principal. He would say to himself that this was a dangerous boy on whom one must keep one's eye. From further inquiry he would find out still more serious things about him: that the boy made blasphemous remarks about God; that he described the priests in language that can scarcely be repeated; that he strongly urged his peers not to put up with any interference, and indeed he even planned to go to the zoological gardens and set free the animals whom he regarded as wrongfully imprisoned there. A conservative teacher of the old school would surely say: The rebelliousness of this boy must definitely be checked before it is too late and before he has become a serious menace to society. A modern educator, on the contrary, might have the highest hopes for this child's future, and would see in him a future leader and liberator of the masses.

I have to tell you that both would be equally mistaken, and that all actions based upon their understanding of the manifest situation would be harmful and false. In reality, this 8-year-old boy was a harmless little coward, in terror when a dog barked at him, frightened to go along a dark corridor in the evening, and certainly not capable of hurting a fly. His rebellious sayings had an unexpected origin. In his early years he was a passionately devoted child and an intense masturbator. This was interfered with by prohibitions and by a necessary surgical intervention which acted as a severe shock. The latter aroused in him immense anxiety and concern for the safety of his genital. As a consequence, he began to battle against any kind of authority. If anybody in this world had power, he felt, then he also had the power to punish and castrate. Consequently every possibility of a heavenly or earthly ruler must be removed from the world. The greater his fear, the more he tried to overcome it by his loud but futile attacks on those in authority.

This noisy method of protecting himself was, moreover, not his only one. Although he acted the part of an atheist, he kneeled down in the evening, and prayed, impelled by fear. He thought: "There is indeed no God. But perhaps after all there might be one, and then it would be a good thing, in any case, to behave properly to Him."

What is important to realize is that this boy was neither a future menace to society nor a future liberator of the masses and that he needed neither admiration nor harshness and restrictions, but only—by some means or other—an abatement of his fears. Only this could release him from his neurotic behavior, and enable him to fulfill his capacity for enjoyment and work as an adult.

The psychoanalytic method of treatment which can achieve this is, thus, the third service that psychoanalysis renders to the upbringing of children. But the description of this therapy, i.e., child analysis, would go far beyond the limits of this course.

Part III
EARLY PAPERS

1

Beating Fantasies and

Daydreams (1922)

In his paper "A Child Is Being Beaten" Freud (1919) deals with a fantasy which, according to him, is met with in a surprising number of persons who seek analytic treatment on account of a hysteria or an obsessional neurosis. He

---

This paper was written following several discussions with Lou Andreas-Salomé. It was first presented to the Vienna Psychoanalytic Society on May 31, 1922. It was published as "Schlagephantasie und Tagtraum" in *Imago*, 8:317–332, 1922. The English translation appeared in the *International Journal of Psycho-Analysis*, 4:89–102, 1923. A Spanish translation entitled "Relacion entre fantasias de flagelacion y sueño diurno" appeared in *Revista de Psicoanálisis*, 4:258–271, 1946. The version presented here has been revised.

thinks it very probable that it occurs even more often in other persons who have not been forced by a manifest illness to come to this decision. This "beating fantasy" is invariably invested with a high degree of pleasure and is discharged in an act of pleasurable autoerotic gratification. I shall take for granted that you are familiar with the content of Freud's paper—the description of the fantasy, the reconstruction of the phases which preceded it, and its derivation from the oedipus complex. In the course of my paper I shall frequently return to it.

In this paper Freud says: "In two of my four female cases an elaborate superstructure of day-dreams, which was of great significance for the life of the person concerned, had grown up over the masochistic beating fantasy. The function of this superstructure was to make possible a feeling of satisfied excitation, even though the masturbatory act was abstained from" (p. 190). I have been able to find one daydream, among a large variety of them, which seemed especially well suited to illustrate this brief remark. This daydream was formed by a girl of about fifteen, whose fantasy life, in spite of its abundance, had never come into conflict with reality. The origin, evolution, and termination of this daydream could be established with certainty, and its derivation from and dependence on a beating fantasy of long standing were proved in a rather thoroughgoing analysis.

I

I shall now trace the development of the fantasy life of this daydreamer. In her fifth or sixth year—the exact date could not be established, but it was certainly before she entered school—this girl formed a beating fantasy of the type described by Freud. In the beginning its content was quite monotonous: "A boy is being beaten by a grownup." Somewhat later is changed to: "Many boys are being beaten by many grownups." The identity of the boys as well as that of the grownups, however, remained unknown, as did in almost all instances the misdeed for which the castigation was administered. We can assume that the various scenes were quite vivid in the child's imagination, but her references to them during the analysis were quite scanty and vague. Each one of the scenes she fantasied, frequently only very briefly, was accompanied by strong sexual excitement and terminated in a masturbatory act.

The sense of guilt which in the case of this girl, too, immediately became attached to this fantasy is explained by Freud in the following way. He says that this version of the beating fantasy is not the original one, but is the substitute in consciousness for an earlier unconscious phase in which the persons who have now become unrecognizable and indifferent were very well known and important: the boy who is being beaten is the child who produced the fantasy; the adult who beats, the child's own father. Yet even this phase is, according to Freud, not the primary one; it was preceded by an earlier phase which belongs to the period of the greatest activity of the oedipus complex and which by means of regression and repression was transformed into the version appearing in the second phase. In the first phase the person who beats also was the father; however, the child who was being beaten was not the fantasying child but other children, brothers or sisters, i.e., rivals for the father's love. In this first phase, therefore, the child claimed all the love for himself and left all the punishment and castigation to the others. With the repression of the oedipal strivings and the dawning sense of guilt, the punishment is subsequently turned back on the child himself. At the same time, however, as a consequence of regression from the genital to the pregenital anal-sadistic organization, the beating situation could still be used as an expression of a love situation. This is the reason for the formation of a second version which because of its all-too-significant content must remain unconscious and be replaced in consciousness by a third version that is more appropriate to the requirements of repression. This is how the third version or phase becomes the carrier of excitement and guilt; for the hidden meaning of this strange fantasy can still be expressed with the words: "Father loves only me."

In the case of our daydreamer the sense of guilt that arose in the wake of her repressed strivings for her father was at first attached less to the content of the fantasy itself— though the latter too was disapproved of from the beginning—than to the autoerotic gratification which regularly occurred at its termination. For a number of years, therefore, the little girl made ever-renewed but ever-failing attempts to separate the one from the other, i.e., to retain the fantasy as a source of pleasure and, at the same time, to give up the sexual gratification which could not be reconciled with the demands of her ego. During this period the fantasy itself was subjected to a great variety of alterations and elaborations. In the attempt to enjoy the permissible pleasure as long as possible and to put off the forbidden conclusion indefinitely, she added all sorts of accessory details that in themselves were quite indifferent but copiously described. The child invented complicated organizations and complete institutions, schools, and reformatories in which the beating scenes were to take place, and established definite rules and regulations which determined the conditions of gaining pleasure. At that time the persons administering the beatings were invariably teachers; only later and in exceptional cases the fathers of the boys were added —as spectators mostly. But even in these detailed elaborations of the fantasy, the acting figures remained schematic, all determining characteristics such as names, individual faces, and personal history being denied to them.

I certainly do not want to imply that such a postponement of the pleasurable scene, the prolongation and continuation of the entire fantasy, is always the expression of guilt feelings, a result of the attempt to separate the fantasy from the masturbatory activity. The same mechanism is used in fantasies which are not shaped by feelings of guilt. In such fantasies this mechanism simply serves the function of heightening the tension and thereby also the anticipated end pleasure.

Let us look at the further vicissitudes of the little girl's beating fantasy. With increasing age there occurred a strengthening of all the tendencies subserving the ego, in which the moral demands of the environment were now incorporated. As a result it became increasingly difficult for the fantasy in which the child's entire sexual life was concentrated to assert itself. She gave up her invariably unsuccessful attempts to separate the beating fantasy from the autoerotic gratification; the prohibition spread and now extended also to the content of the fantasy. Each breakthrough which now could occur only after a prolonged struggle in which strong forces opposed the temptation was followed by violent self-reproaches, pangs of conscience, and temporary depressed moods. The pleasure derived from the fantasy was more and more confined to a single pleasurable moment which seemed to be embedded in unpleasure that occurred before and after it. As the beating fantasy no longer served its function of providing pleasure, it occurred less and less frequently in the course of time.

II

At about the same time—probably between her eighth and tenth year (the exact age again could not be ascertained)— the girl initiated a new kind of fantasy activity which she herself called "nice stories" in contrast to the ugly beating fantasy. These "nice stories" seemed at first sight at least to depict nothing but pleasant, cheery scenes that all exemplify instances of kind, considerate, and affectionate behavior. All the figures in these nice stories had names, individual faces, external appearances that were detailed with great exactness, and personal histories which frequently reached far back into their fantasied past. The family circumstances of these figures, their friendships and acquaintances, and their relationship to each other were precisely specified and all incidents in their daily life were fashioned as true to reality as possible. The setting of the story readily changed with every change in the life of the daydreamer, just as she frequently incorporated bits and pieces of events she had read about. The conclusion of each rounded out episode was regularly accompanied by a strong feeling of happiness unclouded by any trace of guilt; certainly, there no longer was any autoerotic activity connected with it. This type of fantasy activity could therefore take over an ever-increasing part of the child's life. Here we encounter what Freud stressed in his paper: the artistic superstructure of daydreams which are of great significance for the person who forms them. In what follows I shall attempt to demonstrate the extent to which we are justified in regarding these daydreams as a superstructure built on a masochistic beating fantasy.

The daydreamer herself was quite unaware of any connection between the nice stories and the beating fantasy, and at that time would most certainly and without any hesitation have denied it. To her the beating fantasy represented everything that was ugly, reprehensible, and forbidden, while the nice stories were the expression of everything that brought beauty and happiness. A connection between the two simply could not exist; in fact, it was inconceivable that a figure playing a part in a nice story could even appear in the beating scene.

The two were kept apart so carefully that each occurrence of the beating fantasy—which on occasion did break through—had to be punished by a temporary renunciation of the nice stories.

I mentioned earlier that during the analysis the girl gave only the most cursory account of the beating fantasy—usually made with every indication of shame and resistance and in the form of brief, obscure allusions on the basis of which the analyst laboriously had to reconstruct the true picture. In contrast to this reticence, she was only too eager, once the initial difficulties had been overcome, to talk vividly and at length about the various fantasied episodes of her nice stories. In fact, one gained the impression that she never tired of talking and that in doing so she experienced a similar or even greater pleasure than in the daydreaming. In those circumstances it was not difficult to obtain a very clear picture of all the figures and the range of situation. It turned out that the girl had formed not one but a whole series of stories which deserve to be called "continued stories" in view of the constancy of the acting figures and the entire general setting. Among these continued stories one stood out as the most important: it contained the largest number of figures, persisted through the longest period of years, and underwent various transformations. Moreover, from it other stories branched off, which —as in legends and mythology—were elaborated into innumerable almost independent tales. Alongside the main story there existed various minor, more or less important stories which were used in turn but all of which were fashioned according to the same pattern. To gain insight into the structure of such a daydream I have selected as an example the briefest of the nice stories which because of its clarity and completeness is best suited to the purposes of this communication.

In her fourteenth or fifteenth year, after having formed a number of continued daydreams which she maintained side by side, the girl accidentally came upon a boy's storybook; it contained among others a short story set in the Middle Ages. She read through it once or twice with lively interest; when she had finished, she returned the book to its owner and did not see it again. Her imagination, however, was immediately captured by the various figures and their external circumstances which were described in the book. Taking possession of them, she further spun out the tale, just as if it had been her own spontaneous fantasy product, and henceforth accorded this daydream a not insignificant place in the series of her nice stories.

In spite of several attempts that were made during the analysis, it was not possible to establish even approximately the content of the story she had read. The original story had been so cut up into separate pieces, drained of their content, and overlaid by new fantasy material that it was impossible to distinguish between the borrowed and the spontaneously produced elements. All we can do therefore —and that was also what the analyst had to do—is to drop this distinction, which in any event has no practical significance, and deal with the entire content of the fantasied episodes regardless of their sources.

The material she used in this story was as follows: A medieval knight has been engaged in a long feud with a number of nobles who are in league against him. In the course of a battle a fifteen-year-old noble youth (i.e., the age of the daydreamer) is captured by the knight's henchmen. He is taken to the knight's castle where he is held prisoner for a long time. Finally, he is released.

Instead of spinning out and continuing the tale (as in a novel published in installments), the girl made use of the plot as a sort of outer frame for her daydream. Into this frame she inserted a variety of minor and major episodes, each a completed tale that was entirely independent of the others, and formed exactly like a real novel, containing an introduction, the development of a plot which leads to heightened tension and ultimately to a climax. In this she did not feel bound to work out a logical sequence of events. Depending on her mood she could revert to an earlier or later-occurring phase of the tale, or interpose a new situation between two already completed and contemporaneous scenes—until finally the frame of her stories was in danger of being shattered by the abundance of scenes and situations accommodated within it.

In this daydream, which was the simplest of them all, there were only two figures that were really important; all the others can be disregarded as incidental and subordinate by-players. One of these main figures is the noble youth whom the daydreamer has endowed with all possible good and attractive characteristics; the other one is the knight of the castle who is depicted as sinister and violent. The opposition between the two is further intensified by the addition of several incidents from their past family histories—so that the whole setting is one of apparently irreconcilable antagonism between one who is strong and mighty and another who is weak and in the power of the former.

A great introductory scene describes their first meeting during which the knight threatens to put the prisoner on the rack to force him to betray his secrets. The youth's conviction of his helplessness is thereby confirmed and his dread of the knight awakened. These two elements are the basis of all subsequent situations. For example, the knight in fact threatens the youth and makes ready to torture him, but at the last moment the knight desists. He nearly kills the youth through the long imprisonment, but just before it is too late the knight has him nursed back to health. As soon as the prisoner has recovered the knight threatens him again, but faced by the youth's fortitude the knight spares him again. And every time the knight is just about to inflict great harm, he grants the youth one favor after another.

Or let us take another example from a later phase of the story. The prisoner has strayed beyond the limits of his confine and meets the knight, but the latter does not as expected punish the youth with renewed imprisonment. Another time the knight surprises the youth in the very act of transgressing a specific prohibition, but he himself spares the youth the public humiliation which was to be the punishment for this crime. The knight imposes all sorts of deprivations and the prisoner then doubly savors the delights of what is granted again.

All this takes place in vividly animated and dramatically moving scenes. In each the daydreamer experiences the full excitement of the threatened youth's anxiety and fortitude. At the moment when the wrath and rage of the torturer are transformed into pity and benevolence—that is to say, at the climax of each scene—the excitement resolves itself into a feeling of happiness.

The enactment of these scenes in her imagination and the formation of ever new, but very similar scenes usually required a few days, at most some two weeks. The systematic elaboration and development of the single daydream elements usually succeed best at the beginning of each such phase of fantasying. At that time she already made extensive use of the possibility of disregarding the implications and consequences of each situation. As was previously mentioned, she could completely ignore what had happened before or after an incident. As a consequence she was each time fully convinced of the dangers threatening the prisoner and truly believed in the eventual unhappy ending of the scene. We thus see that the events leading to the climax—the preparation for it—were given ample scope. But if the fantasying persisted over a prolonged period of time, memory fragments of happy endings apparently were dragged along from scene to scene, contrary to the day-dreamer's intentions. Then the anxiety and concern for the prisoner were described without real conviction, and the forgiving-loving mood of the climax, instead of being confined to a single brief moment of pleasure, began to spread until it finally also took over all that had previously served the purposes of introduction and development of the plot. But when this happened, the story no longer served its function and had now to be replaced (at least for several weeks) by another which after some time met with the same fate. The only exception was the main great daydream which by far outlasted all the minor insignificant stories. This was probably due to the great wealth of characters appearing in it as well as to its manifold ramifications. Nor is it unlikely that its broad design was carried through for the very purpose of ensuring it a longer life every time it emerged.

If we look at the various separate knight-youth day-dreams as a continuous and connected series, we are surprised by their monotony, though the daydreamer herself never noticed it either in the course of fantasying or in talking about them in the analysis. Yet she was otherwise by no means an unintelligent girl and was in fact quite critical and exacting in the choice of her reading material. But the various scenes of the knight tale, divested of their accessory details which at first glance seemed to give them a vivid and individualized appearance, are in each case constructed on the same scaffold: antagonism between a strong and a weak person; a misdeed—mostly unintentional—on the part of the weak one which puts him at the other's mercy; the latter's menacing attitude which justifies the gravest apprehensions; a slowly mounting anxiety, often depicted by exquisitely appropriate means, until the tension becomes almost unendurable; and finally, as the pleasurable climax, the solution of the conflict, the pardoning of the sinner, reconciliation, and, for a moment, complete harmony between the former antagonists. Every one of the individual scenes of the other so-called "nice stories" had, with only a few variations, the same structure.

But this structure also contains the important analogy between the nice stories and the beating fantasy which our daydreamer did not suspect. In the beating fantasy, too, the protagonists are strong and weak persons who in their clearest delineation oppose each other as adults and children. There, too, it is regularly a matter of a misdeed, even though the latter is left as indefinite as the acting figures. There, too, we find a period of mounting fear and tension. The decisive difference between the two rests in their solution, which in the fantasy is brought about by beating, and in the daydream by forgiveness and reconciliation.

When in the analysis the girl's attention was drawn to these surprising similarities in structure, she could no longer reject the dawning awareness of a connection between these two, externally so different fantasy products. Once she had accepted the probability of their relatedness she immediately was struck by a series of other connections between them.

But despite the acknowledgment of their similar structure, the content of the beating fantasy seemed to have nothing in common with the nice stories. The assertion that their content differed, however, could not really be maintained. Closer observation showed that at various places the nice stories contained more or less clear traces of the old beating theme attempting to break through. The best example of this can be found in the knight daydream with which we already are familiar: the torture that is threatened, though not carried out, constitutes the background of a great number of scenes lending them a distinct coloring of anxiety. This threatened torture, however, is reminiscent of the old beating scene, the execution of which remains forbidden in the nice stories. Other forms of beating breaking through into the daydream can be found, not in this particular tale of the knight, but in other daydreams of this girl.

The following example is taken from the great main story, as far as it was revealed in the analysis. In many scenes the role of the passive, weak person (the youth in the tale of the knight) is enacted by two figures. Though both have the same antecedents, one is punished and the other pardoned. In this instance the punishment scene was neither pleasurably nor unpleasurably accentuated; it simply formed a backdrop to the love scene, their contrast serving to heighten the pleasure.

In another variation of the daydream, the passive person is made to recall all the past punishments he suffered while he is actually being treated affectionately. Here, too, the contrast serves to heighten the pleasurable accent.

In a third version, the active, strong person recalls, just as he is overcome by the conciliatory mood associated with the climax, a past act of punishment or beating which he, having committed the same crime, endured.

The four versions just described illustrate ways in which the beating theme can encroach upon the main theme of a daydream. But it also may be worked out in such a way that it constitutes the most essential theme of a daydream. One of the prerequisites for this is the omission of an element that is indispensable in the beating fantasy, namely, the humiliation in being beaten. Thus the great main story of this girl contained several particularly impressive scenes which culminated in the descriptions of an act of beating or punishment, the former being described as unintentional, the latter as self-punishment.

Each of these examples of the beating theme erupting into the nice stories was furnished by the daydreamer herself, and each could be used as a further proof for the assertion that the two were related. But the most convincing evidence for their relatedness came later in the analysis in the form of a confession. The girl admitted that on some rare occasions a direct reversal of the nice stories into the beating fantasy had taken place. During difficult periods, i.e., at times of increased external demands or diminished internal capabilities, the nice stories no longer succeeded in fulfilling their task. And then it had frequently happened that at the conclusion and climax of a fantasied beautiful scene the pleasurable and pleasing love scene was suddenly replaced by the old beating situation together with the sexual gratification associated with it, which then led to a full discharge of the accumulated excitement. But such incidents were quickly forgotten, excluded from memory, and consequently treated as though they had never happened.

Our investigation of the relationship between beating fantasy and nice stories has so far established three important links: (1) a striking similarity in the construction of the individual stories; (2) a certain parallelism in their content; and (3) the possibility of a direct reversal of one into the other. The essential difference between the two lies in the fact that the nice stories admit the occurrence of unexpected affectionate scenes precisely at the point where the beating fantasy depicts the act of chastisement.

With these points in mind, I return to Freud's reconstruction of the history of the beating fantasy. As already mentioned, Freud says that the form in which we know the beating fantasy is not the original one, but is a substitute for an incestuous love scene that distorted by repression and regression to the anal-sadistic phase finds expression as a beating scene. This point of view suggests an explanation of the difference between beating fantasy and daydream: what appears to be an advance from beating fantasy to nice story is nothing but a return to an earlier phase. Being manifestly removed from the beating scene, the nice stories regain the latent meaning of the beating fantasy: the love situation hidden in it.

But this assertion still lacks an important link. We have learned that the climax of the beating fantasy is inseparably associated with the urge to obtain sexual gratification and the subsequently appearing feelings of guilt. In contrast, the climax of the nice stories is free of both. At first glance this seems to be inexplicable since we know that both sexual gratification and sense of guilt derive from the repressed love fantasy which is disguised in the beating fantasy but represented in the nice stories.

The problem resolves itself when we take into consideration that the nice stories also do not give expression to the repressed love fantasy without changing it. In this incestuous wish fantasy stemming from early childhood all the sexual drives were concentrated on a first love object, the father. The repression of the oedipus complex forced the child to renounce most of his infantile sexual aims. The early "sensual" aims were relegated to the unconscious. That they reemerge in the beating fantasy indicates a partial failure of the attempted repression.

While the beating fantasy thus represents a return of the

repressed, the nice stories on the other hand represent its sublimation. In the beating fantasy the direct sexual drives are satisfied, whereas in the nice stories the aim-inhibited drives, as Freud calls them, find gratification. Just as in the development of a child's relations to his parents, the originally undivided current of love becomes separated into repressed sensual strivings (here expressed in the beating fantasy) and into a sublimated affectionate tie (represented by the nice stories).

The two fantasy products can now be compared in terms of the following scheme: the function of the beating fantasy is the disguised representation of a never-changing sensual love situation which it expresses in the language of the anal-sadistic organization as an act of beating. The function of the nice stories, on the other hand, is the representation of the various tender and affectionate stirrings. Its theme, however, is as monotonous as that of the beating fantasy. It consists in bringing about a friendship between a strong and a weak person, an adult and a boy, or, as many daydreams express it, between a superior and an inferior being.

The sublimation of sensual love into tender friendship is of course greatly facilitated by the fact that already in the early stages of the beating fantasy the girl abandoned the difference of the sexes and is invariably represented as a boy.

III

It was the object of this paper to examine the nature of the relationship between beating fantasies and daydreams which coexisted side by side. As far as possible their mutual dependence could be established. In what follows I shall use the opportunity provided by this case to follow the further development and fate of one of these continued daydreams.

Several years after the story of the knight first emerged, the girl put it in writing. She produced an absorbing short story which covers the period of the youth's imprisonment. It began with the prisoner's torture and ended with his refusal to escape. One suspects that his voluntary choice to remain at the castle is motivated by positive feelings for the knight. All events are depicted as having occurred in the past, the story being presented in the frame of a conversation between the knight and the prisoner's father.

While the written story thus retained the theme of the daydream, the method of its elaboration was changed. In the daydream the friendship between the strong and the weak characters had to be established over and over again in every single scene, while in the written story its development extends over the entire period of the action. In the course of this transformation the individual scenes of the daydream were lost; while some of the situational material that they contained returned in the written story, the individual climaxes were not replaced by a single great climax at the end of the written tale. Its aim—harmonious union between the former antagonists—is only anticipated but not really described. As a result, the interest, which in the daydream was concentrated on specific highpoints, is in the written version divided equally among all situations and protagonists.

This change of structure corresponds to a change in the mechanism of obtaining pleasure. In the daydream each new addition or repetition of a separate scene afforded a new opportunity for pleasurable instinctual gratification. In the written story, however, the direct pleasure gain is abandoned. While the actual writing was done in a state of happy excitement, similar to the state of daydreaming, the finished story itself does not elicit any such excitement. A reading of it does not lend itself to obtaining daydreamlike pleasures. In this respect it had no more effect on its author than the reading of any comparable story written by another person would have had.

These findings suggest a close connection between the two important differences between the daydream and the written story—the abandonment of the individual scenes and the renunciation of the daydreamlike pleasure gain at specific climaxes. The written story must have been motivated by different factors and serve other functions than the daydream. Otherwise the story of the knight would simply have become something unusable in its transformation from fantasy to written story.

When the girl was asked what had induced her to write down the story, she herself could give only one reason of which she was aware. She believed that she had turned to writing at a time when the daydream of the knight was especially obtrusive—that is to say, as a defense against excessive preoccupation with it. She had sought to create a kind of independent existence for the protagonists that had become all too vivid, in the hope that they then would no longer dominate her fantasy life. The daydream of the knight was in fact finished, as far as she was concerned, after it had been written down.

But this account of her motivation still leaves many things unexplained: the very situations that owing to their overvividness are supposed to have impelled her to write down the story are not included in it, whereas others that were not part of the daydream (e.g., the actual torturing) are dwelt on extensively. The same is true with regard to the protagonists: the written story omits several figures whose individual characterization was fully executed in the daydream and instead introduces entirely new ones, such as the prisoner's father.

A second motivation for writing the story can be derived from Bernfeld's observations (1924) of the creative attempts of adolescents. He remarks that the motive of writing down daydreams is not to be found in the daydream itself, but is extrinsic to it. He maintains that such creative endeavors are prompted by certain ambitious tendencies originating in the ego; for example, the adolescent's wish to influence others by poetry, or to gain the respect and love of others by these means. If we apply this theory to the girl's story of the knight, the development from the daydream to the written story may have been as follows:

In the service of such ambitious strivings as have just been mentioned, the private fantasy is turned into a communication addressed to others. In the course of this transformation regard for the personal needs of the daydreamer is replaced by regard for the prospective reader. The pleasure derived directly from the content of the story can be dispensed with, because the process of writing by satisfying the ambitious strivings indirectly produces pleasure in the author. This renunciation of the direct pleasure gain, however, also obviates the need to accord special treatment to certain parts of the story—the climax of the daydreams—which were especially suited to the purpose of obtaining pleasure. Likewise, the written story (as the inclusion of the torture scene demonstrates) can discard the restrictions imposed on the daydream in which the realization of situations stemming from the beating fantasy had been proscribed.

The written story treats all parts of the content of the daydream as equally objective material, the selection being guided solely by regard for their suitability for representation. For the better she succeeds in the presentation of her material, the greater will be the effect on others and therefore also her own indirect pleasure gain. By renouncing her private pleasure in favor of making an impression on others, the author has accomplished an important developmental step: the transformation of an autistic into a social activity. We could say: she has found the road that leads from her fantasy life back to reality.

2

A Hysterical Symptom in a Child of Two Years and Three Months (1923)

The little incident which I shall report here did not come under my observation. The child's mother, Hilda Sissermann, told me about it and gave me leave to publish it.

First published as "Ein hysterisches Symptom bei einem zwei-einviertel jährigen Knaben." *Imago*, 9:264–265, 1923. The English translation first appeared in the *International Journal of Psycho-Analysis*, 7:227–229, 1926.
The version presented here has been revised.

She vouches for the correctness of the observation. Her story is as follows:

At the time the incident occurred she and her children were living in a house with a courtyard in which there was a deep well. She had repeatedly told all the children that they were not to go near the well by themselves or even to play by it and, in order to deter them from doing so, she had vividly described to them the danger of falling in. One day she happened to be standing near the well with one of the children, a little boy of 2¼ years, when a full bucket of water which had just been drawn broke away from the chain and crashed down into the well. The incident obviously made a profound impression on the boy. He spoke of it as follows (as far as he could speak plainly at all): "Bucket was naughty; bucket fell into the well." He continued to talk of it with excitement, making the bucket into a child, and finally he himself became the child that fell in.

After his mother and he had gone back into the house, while she was beginning to take off his little coat, he suddenly began to scream and cry, calling out that his arm hurt him, that they must not touch it, for he had "broken it to bits" when he fell into the well. His mother was convinced that it must be simply a fantasy and tried, first gently and then sternly, to make him obey her, but without success. At last she became frightened at the look of his arm, which he kept rigidly bent, so that the baby fat bulged out all over and made it look swollen. She began to wonder if, in leading him in, she could really have strained or sprained his arm, and so she sent for the doctor.

He was a clever physician, experienced in the ways of

children. He gave it as his opinion that there was no evidence of a fracture, but was inclined to think that there was a very painful strain, and prescribed poultices. While the arm was being examined the child screamed as if in torments. His little coat had been cut away. He was put to bed and sat up in his cot and played, without ever moving his arm; when anyone tried to touch it he screamed. When he was asleep in the afternoon his mother tried to touch the arm, and immediately he woke up. Nevertheless she still felt a doubt about the reality of the injury. When the boy woke up from his afternoon nap, she sat down by his bed with a friend and played with him so long and in such a diverting way that he gradually became more lively and forgot everything, and finally stretched, lifted, turned, and dropped both arms, while playing at being a bird and flying. From that moment nothing more was heard of his arm hurting him.

This is the mother's account, and she adds that in his later development the child never again showed a tendency to symptom formation of this sort.

I think that in this case a large part of the mechanism of symptom formation is plainly evident. Probably the little boy had often wished to disobey his mother and go near the tempting well. On the basis of this wish feelings of guilt arose, which enabled him to put himself in the place of the bucket and to transfer to himself what he imagined to be the bucket's punishment.

But I think we may venture to supplement this with a further stage in the mechanism. We are probably justified in supposing that the feelings of guilt, which related to playing by the well, were reinforced by other, more serious feelings arising from the actual, and not merely fantasied, transgression of a prohibition; I refer to the prohibition of masturbation. If this were so what the child saw happen at the well—the breaking away of the bucket from the chain and its fall into the depths of the water—must have signified to him a symbolic execution of the threat of castration: the loss of a guilty and highly prized bodily organ—first of all the penis itself, and then, by a process of displacement, the arm and the hand which had shared the forbidden activity.

From this point of view the child's symptom had a double meaning. The stiffness and immobility of his arm would represent the influence of moral tendencies, since these symptoms would constitute a direct punishment for masturbation and a renunciation of the habit. The way in which he held his arm tightly pressed to his body and anxiously shielded it from every interference from outside would represent a defense against the instinctual wish and a precautionary measure against the castration which he feared.

Of course, from a distance and without any possibility of testing one's supposition, it is impossible to decide how far the explanation I have suggested is really correct.

3

The Theory of Child
Analysis (1928 [1927])

Ladies and Gentlemen: In recent years the psychoanalysis
of children has attracted greatly increased interest. This is

---

This paper was first presented at the 10th Congress of the International Psycho-Analytical Association Innsbruck 1927, and published as "Zur Theorie der Kinderanalyse," in *Internationale Zeitschrift für Psychoanalyse*, 14:153–162, 1928. It was subsequently
included in the second edition of *Einführung in die Technik der
Kinderanalyse* (1929). The English translation, by Nancy Procter-
Gregg, appeared first in the *International Journal of Psycho-Analysis*,
10:29–38, 1929; it was republished as Part II of *The Psychoanalytical Treatment of Children* (1946) and thereafter appeared in all
subsequent editions and translations of this book (see Publishing
History, pp. xviiff.).
The version presented here has been revised by the author.

mainly due to three factors. It brings welcome confirmation of the conceptions of the mental life of children which psychoanalytic theory has formulated on the basis of reconstructions from adult analysis over the course of years; it supplies new disclosures to round out these ideas from direct observation; and finally it furnishes a transition to a sphere which, as many think, should in the future be one of the most important for psychoanalysis: its application to the upbringing of children.

But, supported by these three claims to be of service, the analysis of children presumes to take various liberties. It calls for a new technique. There can be no real objection to this, for even the most conservative will admit that altered problems must be approached with modified methods. And so there emerges Melanie Klein's play technique for small children, and later the ideas propounded by me for analysis of the latency period. But some exponents of the analysis of children, and I among them, go even further. They are beginning to wonder whether the processes in a child's analysis fully correspond to those in an adult's, and whether the two fully coincide so far as aim and intentions are concerned. They believe that the child analyst—in accord with the fact that his patient is a child—should in addition to the analytic aspect also have a second outlook: the educational. I do not see why we should be frightened of this word, or regard such a combination of two attitudes as a disparagement of analysis. It may be worthwhile to test the validity of this view in the light of some examples.

I select as my first example a fragment from the analysis of an 11-year-old boy. When he began treatment, he was a passive-feminine character, his original object relationship with his mother being entirely overlaid by identification with her. His original masculine aggressiveness found expression only occasionally in hostile behavior to his brothers and sisters and in isolated delinquent acts, which were followed by violent fits of repentance and depression. In this period of his analysis he was preoccupied, in numerous ideas, fantasies, and dreams, with the problem of death, or rather with the infliction of death.

At that time one of his mother's closest friends was very ill, and one day his mother received a telegram saying that her condition was dangerous. He seized on this event, spinning elaborate fantasies around it. He imagined that a new telegram arrived saying she was dead. His mother was extremely grieved. Then came another telegram—she is still alive, it was a mistake. The mother rejoiced. And then he fancied telegrams arriving in quick succession, an announcement of death always followed by another of revival. The fantasy ended with the news that the whole thing was a joke which someone had played on his mother. It is not difficult to interpret; we see his ambivalence clearly expressed, the wish to kill the person loved by his mother, and the inability to pursue his idea to its real conclusion.

Shortly thereafter he reported the following compulsive action. When sitting in the lavatory he had to touch a knob which he found in the wall at one side three times; but then he had to repeat the process at once with a knob on the other side. This action seemed at first unintelligible, until the explanation was found next day through a fantasy recounted in another connection. He imagined God as an old man, seated in the heavenly abode on a big throne. To right and left of him were knobs or switches protruding from the wall. If he pressed the knobs on one side, someone died; if he pressed one on the other, a child came into the world. I trust that linking the compulsive action with the daydream makes further interpretation superfluous. The number 3 is probably to be explained by the number of his brothers and sisters.

Soon afterward another friend of the family fell ill. He was both close to the boy's mother and the father of one of his playmates. The boy heard the telephone ring just as he was leaving for his session with me, and in the session constructed the following fantasy: His mother had been told that she must go to the invalid's house; she went there, entered the sickroom, went up to the bed, wanting to talk with the patient. But he made no reply, and she saw that he was dead. It was a great shock to her. At that moment the dead man's little son came in. She called him and said, "Come here, look, your father is dead." The boy came up to the bed and spoke to his father. The father was alive and answered him. He turned to my patient's mother and said, "What is the matter? He is alive." Then she spoke again to the father, but again he made no reply and was dead. But when the boy came up again and spoke, the father was alive again.

This fantasy is instructive and transparent, and in addition contains the interpretation of the two previous ones. We see that the father is dead in his relationship to the mother, but alive so far as concerns his relationship with the son. While in the previous fantasies the ambivalence— the wish to kill and to bring to life again—was directed to the same person, though split into two different actions which must cancel each other out, the present fantasy gives us the historical elucidation of the double attitude by specifying the person who is threatened—a man, on the one hand, and a father, on the other.

The two tendencies clearly spring from different phases of the boy's development. The death wish against the father as the rival for the mother's love derives from the normal oedipal phase with its since-repressed positive object love for the mother. Here his masculine aggression turns against the father; he must be eliminated, to leave the way free for the child himself. But the other tendency, the wish to retain the father, stems on the one hand from the early period of the purely admiring and loving attitude to the father, undisturbed as yet by the rivalry of the oedipus complex; and on the other hand from the phase—which here plays the more important part—of identification with the mother, which had replaced the normal oedipal attitude. Owing to his fear of castration, threatening from the father, the boy had surrendered his love for the mother and allowed himself to be forced into the feminine attitude. From then on he had to try to sustain the father as an object of his homosexual love.

It would be tempting to go further and describe the transition in the boy from this wish to kill to a fear of death, which manifested itself each evening; and so to find a key to the complicated structure of this neurosis of the latency period. But I have mentioned this fragment only to show that this part of the analysis of a child differs in no way from that of an adult. We have to free a part of this boy's masculine aggressiveness and his object love for his mother from repression and from the overlay by the present passive-feminine character and mother identification. The conflict involved is an inner one. While the fear of his real father in the external world originally drove him into carrying out the repression, the success of this achievement depends for its maintenance upon inner forces. The father has been internalized, the superego has become the representative of his power, and the fear of him is felt by the boy as castration anxiety. At every step which the analysis takes on the path toward making conscious the repressed oedipal tendencies, it encounters outbreaks of this castration anxiety as an obstacle. Only the laborious historico-analytic dissolution of this superego permits the work of liberation to progress. Thus you see that the therapist's work and attitude are, so far as this part of the problem is concerned, purely analytic. There is no place here for any educational admixture.

But in contrast listen to another example, this time from the analysis of a 6-year-old obsessional little girl (whom I have mentioned several times in Part I of this volume). In her case as well—as always—we are dealing with the impulses of the oedipus complex, and here again the idea of killing plays a part. The little girl had, as the analysis disclosed, gone through a period of early passionate love for her father, and in the usual way had been disappointed in him by the birth of the next sibling. Her reaction to that was extraordinarily strong. She surrendered the barely achieved genital phase in favor of a full regression to anal sadism. She turned her hostility against the new arrival. Having turned her love almost completely away from her father, she made an effort to retain him at least by incorporation. But her endeavors to feel herself a man came to naught in the rivalry with an elder brother, whom she recognized to be better equipped bodily for this role. The result was an intensified hostility toward the mother—hatred of her, because she had taken the father from her; hatred, because she had not made her a boy; and, finally, hatred, because she had borne the child whom my little patient herself would willingly have brought into the world.

But at this point—somewhere in her fourth year—something decisive occurred. She perceived dimly that through these hate reactions she was about to lose entirely any good relationship to her mother whom from early childhood on she had after all loved dearly. And in order to rescue her love for her mother, and still more her mother's love for her without which she could not live, she made a mighty effort to be "good." She split off, as it were with one stroke, all these hatreds, and with them her whole sexual life with its anal and sadistic habits and fantasies; and set them in opposition to her own personality as something foreign to it, no longer belonging to it, something "devilish."

What was left behind was not much: a diminished and restricted personality whose emotional life was not fully at her disposal, and whose great intelligence and energy were occupied in forcefully keeping the "devil" in the state of repression imposed on it. Very little indeed was left for the outside world: she had at best only lukewarm feelings of tenderness toward her mother, not strong enough to bear even the slightest strain, and otherwise an almost complete lack of interest.

In addition, however, even with the greatest expenditure of energy, she was not capable of maintaining this split. The devil occasionally overpowered her for a short time, so that it might happen that without any real external reason she would throw herself down on the floor and shriek, in a fashion which in earlier times would certainly have been deemed "possessed"; or she would suddenly yield and revel with full satisfaction in sadistic fantasies, imagining that she wandered through her parent's house from top to bottom smashing all that she found and throwing the pieces out of the window, and striking off the heads of all the people she met. Such victories of the devil were always followed by anxiety and remorse.

But the split-off evil had yet another way of manifesting itself, even more dangerous. The "devil" liked excrement and dirt; she herself began gradually to develop a particular anxiety as to the punctilious observance of the precepts of cleanliness. Beheading was a matter dear to the devil's heart; she then at a certain time in the morning had to creep to the beds of her brothers and sisters to ascertain whether they were all still alive. The devil transgressed every human law with zest and relish; she, however, developed a fear of earthquakes which came on in the evenings before going to sleep—for someone had given her the idea that earthquakes are the most effective means God uses to punish people on the earth.

Thus her daily life was increasingly taken up with reaction formations, acts of contrition, and reparation for the deeds of the split-off wickedness. We might say that the ambitiously conceived and urgent effort to retain her mother's love and to be socially conforming and "good" had failed miserably; it had simply resulted in an obsessional neurosis.

But I have not claimed your attention for this infantile neurosis because of its fine structure and its unusual sharpness, for this early age. I have described it because of a particular circumstance which emerged during the therapeutic work.

In the case of the 11-year-old boy the motor force of the repression was castration anxiety relating to the father; naturally this castration anxiety also operated as the main resistance in the analysis. But in the analysis of the little girl a different factor was at work. The repression, or rather the splitting of the child's personality, had come into being under the pressure of fear of loss of love. This anxiety must have been very intense, to have such a disturbing effect on the child's whole life. Nevertheless, in the analysis this motivating anxiety did not operate as a serious resistance. Under the impact of my never-changing friendly interest the little patient began to disclose her "bad" side to me quite calmly and naturally. You may think that that was nothing out of the way. Often enough we meet adult patients who anxiously conceal their symptoms from the world, and begin to disclose them only in the secure and uncritical atmosphere of analysis; who, indeed, often recognize them only there for the first time. But this refers only to the description of the symptoms; the friendly interest and the absence of expected criticism never suffice to induce alteration of them.

This, however, was precisely what happened in the case of the little girl. When to my interest and lack of condemnation there was added a relaxation of the strict demands of the parental home, there suddenly occurred a most interesting change: the anxiety was transformed into the wish that it concealed; the reaction formation into the warded-off instinct; and the precautions into the underlying threats to kill. Yet the fear of loss of love, which we should have expected to reemerge under such conditions, was hardly manifest at all. If anything, resistance from that cause was slighter than from any other. It was as though the little girl were saying, "If you do not think it so bad, then I do not either." And with this diminution of the demands she made on herself she gradually accomplished, in the course of the analysis, a progressive reincorporation of all the impulses which previously she had rejected with such great expenditure of energy: the incestuous love for her father, the masculine wish, the death wishes against siblings, and the awareness of her infantile sexual wishes. This progress was halted for a time only by a single serious resistance when she encountered what seemed to her the worst of all—the acknowledgment of the death wish directed against her mother.

That is not the behavior which we have learned to expect from a proper superego. We have learned from the adult neurotic how inaccessible to reason the superego is, how steadfastly it resists every attempt at external influence, and how it will not consent to modify its demands until we have historically dissected it in analysis and traced back every single command and prohibition to the identification with one of the persons who loomed large and were loved in childhood.

I believe that here we have come upon the main and most important difference between the analysis of adults and that of children. In the analysis of adults we are dealing with a situation in which the superego has achieved full independence and is no longer subject to external influences. Here our sole task is to raise all the strivings which contributed to the formation of the neurotic conflict to the same level by bringing them into consciousness. On this new conscious level the conflict can then be dealt with in new ways and brought to a different solution.

In the analysis of children, however, we deal with situations where the superego has not yet achieved full independence; where it operates all too clearly for the sake of those from whom it received its commands, the parents and persons in charge of the child, and is swayed in its demands by every change in the relationship with these people and by all the alterations that may occur in their own outlook. As in the case of adults, we work by purely analytic means with children insofar as we attempt to lift the repressed parts of the id and ego from the unconscious. But our task with the childish superego is a double one. It is analytic and proceeds from within in the historical dissolution of the superego, so far as it is already an independent structure, but it is also educational (in the widest sense of that word) in exercising influences from without, by modifying the relations with those who are bringing up the child, by creating new impressions, and revising the demands made on the child by the environment.

Let us return once again to my little obsessional patient. Had she not come under treatment as a 6-year-old, her infantile neurosis might perhaps, like so many others, have cleared up spontaneously. As heir to it she certainly would have erected a strict superego, which would have presented rigid demands to the ego and would have opposed a difficult-to-overcome resistance to any later analysis. But the view which I put forward is that this strict superego stands at the outcome and not at the inception of the infantile neurosis.

As a further illustration of what I have said I refer to a communication which M. Wulff (1927) has published. He reports phobic attacks of anxiety in a little girl only 1½ years old. In this case the child's parents had tried too early to enforce their cleanliness demands. The little girl could not come up to their requirements and became upset, fearing that she would be sent away. Her anxiety became acute in the dark or when there were unfamiliar sounds, for example, when someone knocked at the door. She constantly asked whether she was good and kept repeating the plea not to be sent away. The worried parents turned to Wulff for advice.

The interesting point about this early symptom is that the infant's anxiety, which Wulff at once recognized as fear of loss of love, is in no way distinguishable from the guilt feelings of an adult neurotic. Must we, however, in this case give credence to so early a development of conscience, and thus of the superego?

Wulff explained to the parents that their little daughter obviously was unable to comply with their demands for sphincter control and advised them to postpone toilet training for the present. They were understanding enough to comply; they explained to the child that they still loved her when she wetted herself, and they tried whenever that happened to allay her fears with renewed assurances of their love. The result, as described by Wulff, was striking. After a few days the child was calm and free of anxiety.

Such therapy is of course possible only very rarely and only with very small children. I do not want to suggest that it is generally applicable. Rather, what Wulff carried out here might be regarded as a therapeutic experiment, one to demonstrate which forces were at the root of the anxiety. If the child's anxiety had been due to excessive superego demands, the parents' reassurances would not have had any influence on her symptom. If, however, the cause of her anxiety was fear of the displeasure of her real, living parents, and not of their internalized images, then it is easy to understand that the symptom could be removed. Wulff had in fact removed the cause of the anxiety.

The superego's accessibility to influence during the early years accounts for many of the direct modifications which can be brought about in the behavior of young children. Through the good offices of Ferenczi, I have had access to the notes of a teacher in a modern American school, the Walden School. This analytically trained teacher describes how neurotic children from strict homes, who come to school while still of kindergarten age, after a first period of surprise and suspicion become acclimatized to the free atmosphere and gradually lose their neurotic symptoms, which are usually reactions to the prohibition of masturbation.

A similiar result would be impossible in the case of an adult neurotic. The freer the surroundings into which he is transplanted, the stronger the fears of his drives, his neurotic defense reactions, and his symptoms. The demands which his superego makes upon him are no longer open to influence from his surroundings. In contrast, once the child has begun to lower his superego demands, he is apt to go to extremes, and to indulge himself further than even the freest environment is ready to permit. Even when liberated he cannot dispense with some limiting influences from the external world.

In conclusion, one more example. A little while ago I overheard a conversation between a 5-year-old boy and his mother. The child had taken a fancy to horses and very much wished to own a live one; his mother on good grounds opposed the fulfillment of his desire. "It doesn't matter," said he, not at all cast down, "I'll wish for it for my next birthday." His mother told him that even then he could not have it. "Then I'll wish for it at Christmas," he said, "one gets everything then." "No, not even at Christmas," said his mother, trying to disabuse him. "Well it still doesn't matter," said he triumphantly, "I shall buy it myself, *for I allow myself to have it.*" This is a clear illustration of the conflict which arises when an inner permission is confronted by a prohibition from without. Some children will adapt to frustration; if they fail to do so, the outcome may be rebellion, delinquency, or neurosis.

Now one more word about the "educational" function of the child analyst. Since we have found that the forces with which we have to contend in the cure of an infantile neurosis are not only internal, but linked to external sources as well, we have a right to require that the child analyst should also assess the child's external situation, not only the internal one. For this part of his task, however, the child analyst needs some basic knowledge of the upbringing of children in general. This will enable him to assess and criticize the influences which have an impact on the child's development; and, if it should prove necessary, to take the child's upbringing out of the hands of those in authority, and for the period of the analysis be in charge of it himself.

4

Psychoanalysis and the Up-bringing of the Young Child (1934 [1932])

In the preceding paper Bernfeld (1934) discussed several aspects of the psychology of the young child without stating how this knowledge should be applied. He probably relied on the fact that for decades teachers have always followed up each new trend in psychological thought in the hope of finding a way out of their difficulties.

This paper was first presented at a Congress of Early Childhood Educators in 1932. The other participants representing the analytic point of view were Siegfried Bernfeld and Gertrud Behn-Eschenburg. The three lectures were intended for educators "most of whom had

We are all aware of the difficult position in which the teacher finds himself. To be sure, we frequently hear it stated that one of the most important community tasks is given over to the teachers, that the most valuable material at the disposal of society comes under their control, that they determine the destiny of the coming generation, but in actual practice we find little of this high value placed on education or on the educator himself. Nor are teachers even so well paid as, let us say, industrialists and bankers, who handle the material resources of the nation. As members of the community the teachers must struggle continually for the esteem of their fellowmen and for recognition from the parents and officials of their district. Although many people believe that the younger the child the more important is his education, in actual practice the valuation of the teacher increases with the age of the pupil. Compare, for example, the esteemed position of the high school teacher or college professor with the status of the kindergarten teacher. There is an inconsistency somewhere.

Usually, however, there is some justification for what is

---

no previous knowledge of the subject; and their purpose was to present in the simplest possible form the fundamental principles of the psychoanalytic theory of the child's development, with particular reference to the possibilities of application of this theory in the field of child training. Analysts accordingly must not be surprised to find, in their perusal of these two lectures, that they add nothing to their knowledge of psychoanalysis" (A. Freud, 1935, p. 1).

First published as "Die Erziehung des Kleinkindes vom psychoanalytischen Standpunkt aus." *Zeitschrift für psychoanalytische Pädagogik*, 8:17–25, 1934; also in *Almanach der Psychoanalyse*. Vienna: Internationaler Psychoanalytischen Verlag 1935, pp. 73–86. The English translation, "Psychoanalysis and the Training of the Young Child" by Julia Deming, was first published in *The Psychoanalytic Quarterly*, 4:15–24, 1935.

The version included here has been revised.

found in actual practice. The low valuation of teachers in general arises from the fact that they are really not independent producers but middlemen, agents, buffers between two generations. They are given raw material and are expected to turn out certain specific products. The only freedom given them is in the choice of pedagogical method. Just because they enjoy so little freedom in other ways, they seize upon this little piece of independence and create out of it the fiction of a great power.

Let us consider another aspect. I think we have the right to assume, that, by and large, the raw material which teachers receive is fairly uniform. The end product desired of them, however, varies enormously according to the period and the type of society in which they work. We need only glance over the history of education to realize what a great variety of products have been demanded in different ages: warlike young Spartans, Athenians devoted to the fine arts, humble ascetics needed by the Church of the Middle Ages, heroic knights or nobles, loyal subjects, good and industrious citizens, fearless revolutionaries, and peace-loving workers.

There is nothing remarkable in these demands. In each instance they express the contemporary needs of an adult society. What is remarkable, however, is the fact that in every period educators have thrown themselves into their task with the same zeal. Let us suppose that the workers in a factory were expected to produce from the same raw material cannon balls in times of war and featherbeds in times of peace. I do not believe that the workers would be as enthusiastic as the teachers have been under comparable conditions.

This enthusiasm of the teacher in trying to meet these most varied demands of society works to his disadvantage in another way. The failures in educational work have always been attributed to the teachers. Society has assumed that the goal was attainable. Consequently it has seemed that somehow the individual teacher was at fault rather than education as a whole.

I believe, indeed, that the reason why teachers in all ages have turned to the science of psychology has been to exonerate themselves from the imputed disgrace of this failure. Psychology, they thought, would teach them the nature of the raw material given over to them. The truth is that teachers will not be in a more favorable position in relation to their employers, i.e., society, until psychology really succeeds in understanding children, the raw material of education. Only then will they be able to point out the discrepancy between the goal set up by society and the capacity of the child to reach this goal. Only then will they weigh the psychological potentialities of the individual child against the demands made on him by society as factors deserving equal consideration. Only when it becomes clear which educational goals are compatible with mental health and which are attainable only at the expense of this health will greater justice be done the child.

Education has obviously two cardinal functions. We can summarize one of them under the caption "allowing and forbidding," by which we mean the educator's behavior toward the spontaneous expressions of the child. The other function concerns the building up of the child's personality. Psychology will have achieved what education has a right to expect of it if, on the one hand, it describes the primitive nature of the child, and, on the other hand, opens up new avenues for possible development and offers new techniques for the further expansion of the child's personality.

Bernfeld concerned himself in detail with the first of these functions. He pictured the child's mental life as made up of instinctual wishes derived from the sexual instinct. These instinctual wishes pass through various phases and change from one form into another; how great a part education plays in this development we do not know. Bernfeld left it an open question what the teacher's attitude should be toward the various instinctual wishes; he merely indicated in a general way that the teacher should respect them.

This attitude of respect, however, is nothing new. Among educators there have long been two different points of view regarding the child's mental life. One of them claims that whatever the child has as native endowment is good. We must respect it and leave it alone, a point of view which Rousseau formulated and which in modern education is sponsored especially by Montessori. According to this attitude the child is always right in what he wants; adults only cause trouble when they interfere.

Far more widely accepted is the other point of view: the child is always in the wrong. The extreme of this is illustrated by a well-known anecdote. A mother says to her nursemaid: "Go and see what the children are doing and tell them to stop."

Actually there is justification for both of these attitudes toward the instinctual impulses of the child. We really should think of instinctual impulses as forces of nature, which the child not only has a right to express but cannot help expressing. Does this mean that we should always sanction these impulses and allow them free rein? It may indeed by argued that just because these impulses are forces of nature and not simply harmless habits or misdemeanors which are relatively easy for the teacher to overcome, we must put forth all our energy to gain mastery over them.

If we introduce our knowledge of the unconscious contents to education without giving specific suggestions for their application, we shall see that this brings us no further than we were before. Instead of letting our feelings determine our attitude toward the child's instincts let us turn again to the psychoanalytic work itself. In the treatment of adults we learn to recognize various types of illness. From each type we can draw conclusions about definite relationships which existed between the child and the persons responsible for his upbringing.

We meet with neurotic inhibitions, for instance, which have developed as a result of one of the instinctual impulses having been forcibly repressed at a very early period, thereby having been entirely prevented from gaining satisfaction. But the impulse is too powerful and tenacious to be quelled in this manner. It continues to make itself felt. An inner conflict arises and eventually the repressed impulse forces its way to the surface, usually in a curiously distorted and disturbing form. But the pathway to direct satisfaction of the instinctual drive in its primitive form remains blocked even after the child has grown up, the external conditions have been changed, and society would now grant what it originally prohibited.

On the other hand, we meet with pathological conditions, such as perversions and certain forms of dissociality which are characterized by an adherence or a regression to an infantile type of instinctual gratification, to the exclusion of all other forms of gratification. In the history of such an illness we usually find a specific event, for instance, seduction, a suddenly overwhelming experience or other traumatic events, which have allowed the particular instinctual impulse to break through and achieve complete gratification. The child's libidinal development remains fixated at this point and does not progress to the desired adult level of instinctual life. These two entirely different types of illness, however, have something in common. In both the child has been caught and held at an infantile level of development, with the result that what should have been only a way station has become a final destination.

Thus we see that a fixation and subsequent neurotic illness may occur either when the impulse is allowed full expression, or, conversely, when it is entirely denied expression. The path to mental health lies somewhere between these two extremes. Evidently the problem is to find a middle course. The instinctual urge must neither be driven into repression, thus preventing its sublimation, i.e., its diversion into other and acceptable channels, nor must it be allowed full satisfaction. It is as if we had to teach the child not to put his hand into the fire because it burns, but dare not express it so directly, lest he become afraid of all fire and be unable in later life to light a match, smoke a cigarette or cook a meal. Our task is to teach the child to keep away from the fire without arousing in him a horror of it.

We can learn something from this simple analogy. If complete instinctual gratification is dangerous for the child, we may be sure that educators have always found frightening the child to be the easiest way out of the situation. For the educators were aware of the dangers of instinctual gratification long before they had any formal knowledge of the child's instinctual drives. By demanding complete renunciation they have made it easy for themselves. They have set limits which the child has not dared to overstep and have utilized every means in their power to reinforce these prohibitions. They have taken advantage of the child's helplessness and weakness in relation to the adult, of his dependence and inability to maintain himself in the external world, in short, they have taken advantage of his fear. In order to avoid a continued struggle with the child and to make it unnecessary to cry out each time he approached the fire of instinctual gratification, "Not this time," they have said, "Once and for all, that burns!" This has apparently been the simplest solution.

How can the intelligent educator of today find the correct solution? Instead of issuing a prohibition, once and for all, the educator must perhaps be prepared for the continued struggle and must lend a helping hand each time the child approaches such an instinctual danger. What means should he use to avoid creating a lasting fear in the child and yet protect him in each individual instance? In the face of this dilemma how can the modern educator carry out the liberal methods which are expected of him? How should he go about it? It is difficult, for denials and prohibitions would seem to be the basis of the young child's training. If this be so, it makes little difference how strict the individual educator may be for the child will experience the very denial of gratification as strictness.

Here again there are two ways of looking at the problem. We may say, on the one hand, that whatever we do, the child is going to feel that he is denied and forbidden all satisfactions, so why should we try to avoid being stern? On the other hand, we may say that no matter how much a child may be spared, he still has to be subjected to a great deal, so why not at least reduce our interference to the minimum? But the fact is that we do struggle with the child over his instinctual gratifications. We want him to have control over his sexual drives, for if they are constantly breaking through, there is the danger that his development will be retarded or arrested, that he will be content with gratifying himself instead of sublimating, with masturbating instead of learning, that he will confine his quest for knowledge to sexual matters instead of extending it to the whole wide world. This we want to prevent.

The situation would really be hopeless for education and for our relations to the little child if he were interested in nothing but the search for pleasure or instinctual gratification from his own body. These powerful active forces operating within the child can be counteracted only by a powerful restraint from without. However, the course of development itself helps to remedy the situation. The period in which the child tries to satisfy his instinctual wishes exclusively on his own person is a relatively short one, whether these wishes be oral, anal, or sadistic. The instinctual impulses soon turn toward the outer world. The child seeks out the people in his immediate environment who are most important to him and insistently demands of them the gratification of his wishes. This is what we call the oedipus situation. We say that the child now has a love object. The peak of this early development is reached when the greater part of his search after pleasure is no longer directed toward his own person but toward an object in the outer world and, above all, when it is concentrated on a single object, the mother or the father.

It would be a great mistake to suppose that this has simplified the child's situation. By turning his impulses toward an outside object he has only complicated matters to an extraordinary degree. In the very earliest period, which we call the autoerotic period, the child's instinctual life pursues an independent course. Only disturbances from the outside are experienced as unpleasant interferences. The child is independent, self-contained, and able to satisfy the demands he makes on himself. But as soon as an external love object is introduced, the child becomes dependent on the goodwill of this object. The satisfaction of every single wish now depends on the consent of the loved being. For instance, the child who has been accustomed to a certain amount of satisfaction from the bodily care given him by his mother must experience a sudden disappointment when she turns him over to the care of someone else who cannot take her place as a love object, thereby depriving him of the possibility of gratification. That is, the child is constantly being threatened, not only with interference from the outer world, but also with rejection at the hands of the love object.

Although for the child the situation has thus been complicated, it has been vastly improved for his training and education. Suppose one and the same person combines the roles of training the child and being his love object. In this case there is little danger that the instinctual drives will break through. The love object needs only to refuse cooperation and renunciation will ensue. The upbringing of the child is therefore incomparably easier during the stage of object love than during the autoerotic phase.

We have already pointed to the child's fear as an aid in his training and education. The earliest fears of being left alone and helplessly exposed to the dangers of the outer world tend to make the child obedient at first. With his attachment to a love object, he experiences a new kind of fear, that of losing this person's love if he fails to obey. So we see that the educator's tools increase in number as the child grows older. The adult can threaten him physically, he can leave him, he can threaten to withdraw his love; and he can do all of these things as punishment for the child's disobedience or refusal to give up his instinctual pleasures.

The situation for the educator becomes progressively easier. Let us recall how hard it is for an adult to give up a love object on whom he has lavished all his affection, on whom he has hoped not only to gratify every single wish, but whom he also desired to possess completely and, if possible, without rivals. When such a person withdraws, this cannot be but a great shock to the one who is deserted. We find that we are actually unable to free ourselves of the unfaithful object, and although to all outward appearances he has left us, deep within us we find him in all sorts of memory traces; yes, even more than that, we find that we ourselves become more like the object, as if we would say, "Even if you have deserted me in the real world, I have retained your image in myself."

If this can happen to an adult, that is to say, a more or less independent and mature being whose personality is fully formed, we can imagine what the small child must go through in similar circumstances. The child of whom we are speaking is in that stage of development in which all his physical wishes, everything that we call sexual, all his aggressions, and also all his love and tenderness are concentrated on one person, on the love object of the oedipus situation. Every child then has the same experience: this love object (the mother) will not or cannot belong to him. She offers him occasional satisfaction, tenderness, and care, but never exclusive possession. The child must consent to share her with his brothers and sisters, must recognize that she belongs in the first place to the father. He must learn to renounce the idea of exclusive possession and all that that means to him.

As a result the child now goes through such a process of extensive self-modification as we described for the adult who loses his love object. That is to say, the child can internally give up his adult love object only at a great price: he must at least partially incorporate the object and modify himself to resemble his mother or father. Strangely enough the child takes over from the object the very things which were most unpleasant and disturbing to him, the commands and the prohibitions. Thus it comes about that toward the end of the oedipus situation, the child, although in part he remains what he has previously been, now carries within himself another part: that of the object and educator. The educator within the child, i.e., this incorporated part—the part with which the child has identified himself, as we express it—now internally treats the other part of the child's personality in the same way as the parental object actually treated the child. This part assumes such an outstanding and overwhelming position in the child's inner life that psychoanalysis has given it a special name. We call it the "superego." It dominates the child's ego just as the parents previously dominated the child.

The formation of the superego facilitates matters for those who are training and educating the child. Whereas up to this point they have carried on the struggle with a being absolutely opposed to them, they now have an ally in the enemy's camp. The educator of the older child can rely on this superego to support him, he knows that he and the superego will join forces against the child. Thus the child finds himself confronted by two authorities, the transformed part of his own personality and his love object who is still present in reality. This docile obedience which we thus create—and which the educators bent on making their task easier often produce to an excessive degree—is precisely what drives the child to excessive repression of instinctual drives and thus into neurosis.

The mechanism described here, more than any other, determines the modification and structure of the child's personality. It proceeds from love for an object to identification with this object. The circumstances arising from this and the further education which is carried on with the assistance of the child's newly established superego are extremely interesting but go beyond the scope of this discussion. The child with a budding or to a certain extent developed superego is no longer a small preschool child; he has entered the second period of childhood, and has passed from the jurisdiction of the parents or preschool educators into the hands of other teachers who undoubtedly have the easier task. The educator of the small child has the most difficult and the most complicated task, but—and here I can only repeat the same consolation that has always been held out to those who raise small children—he also accomplishes the task that determines the future.

Bibliography

AICHHORN, A. (1925), *Wayward Youth*. New York: Viking Press, 1935.

—— (1930), The Juvenile Court: Is It a Solution? In: *Delinquency and Child Guidance*. New York: International Universities Press, 1964, pp. 55–79.

—— (1932), Erziehungsberatung. Z. *psychoanal. Päd.*, 6:445–488.

—— (1936), On the Technique of Child Guidance. In: *Delinquency and Child Guidance*. New York: International Universities Press, 1964, pp. 101–192.

ANGEL, A., *see* Katan, A.

BALINT, A. (1931), *The Early Years of Life*. New York: Basic Books, 1954.

—— (1936), Versagen und Gewähren in der Erziehung. Z. *psychoanal. Päd.*, 10:75–83.

—— (1937), Die Grundlagen unseres Erziehungssystems. Z. *psychoanal. Päd.*, 11:98–101.

BEHN–ESCHENBURG, G. (1934), Die Erziehung des Kleinkind-Erziehers. Z. *psychoanal. Päd.*, 8:26–32.

BERGMANN, T. (1937), Versuch der Behebung einer Erziehungsschwierigkeit. Z. psychoanal. Päd., 11:29–43.

BERNFELD, S. (1922), Kinderheim Baumgarten. Berlin: Jüdischer Verlag.

——— (1924), Vom dichterischen Schaffen der Jugend. Vienna & Leipzig: Internationaler psychoanalytischer Verlag.

——— (1925a), Sisyphos oder die Grenzen der Erziehung. Vienna: Internationaler psychoanalytischer Verlag.

——— (1925b), The Psychology of the Infant. London: Kegan Paul, 1929.

——— (1934), The Psychoanalytic Psychology of the Young Child. Psychoanal. Quart., 4:3–14, 1935.

——— (1935), Über die einfache männliche Pubertät. Z. psychoanal. Päd., 9:360–379.

BORNSTEIN, B. (1930a), Zur Psychogenese der Pseudodebilität. Int. Z. Psychoanal., 16:378–399.

——— (1930b), Beziehung zwischen Sexual- und Intellektentwicklung. Z. psychoanal. Päd., 4:446–454.

——— (1931), Phobia in a Two-and-a-Half-Year-Old Child. Psychoanal. Quart., 4:93–119, 1935.

——— (1934), Enuresis und Kleptomanie als passageres Symptom. Z. psychoanal. Päd., 8:229–237.

——— (1936), Ein Beispiel für die Leugnung durch die Phantasie. Z. psychoanal. Päd., 10:269–275.

——— (1945), Clinical Notes on Child Analysis. The Psychoanalytic Study of the Child, 1:151–166.

BORNSTEIN, S. (1933), A Child Analysis. Psychoanal. Quart., 4:190–225, 1935.

——— (1934), Eine Technik der Kinderanalyse bei Kindern mit Lernhemmungen. Z. psychoanal. Päd., 8:141–154.

——— (1937), Missverständnisse in der psychoanalytischen Pädagogik. Z. psychoanal. Päd., 11:81–90.

BRAUN, E. (1936), Eine Kinderfreundschaft: Beobachtung aus einem Kindergarten. Z. psychoanal. Päd., 10:84–92.

BRIEHL, M. H. (1937), Die Rolle des Märchens in der Klein-kinderziehung. Z. psychoanal. Päd., 11:5–19.

BURLINGHAM, D. (1932), Child Analysis and the Mother. Psychoanal. Quart., 4:69–92, 1935.

—— (1937), Problems Confronting the Psychoanalytic Educator. In: Psychoanalytic Studies of the Sighted and the Blind. New York: International Universities Press, 1972, pp. 71–79.

—— (1939), Fantasy and Reality in a Child's Analysis. In: Psychoanalytic Studies of the Sighted and the Blind. New York: International Universities Press, 1972, pp. 80–94.

BUXBAUM, E. (1934), Exhibitionistic Onanism in a Ten-Year-Old Boy. Psychoanal. Quart., 4:161–189.

—— (1936a), The Role of Detective Stories in a Child Analysis. Psychoanal. Quart., 10:373–381, 1941.

—— (1936b), Massenpsychologie und Schule. Z. psychoanal. Päd., 10:215–240.

ERIKSON, E. H. (1935), Psychoanalysis and the Future of Education. Psychoanal. Quart., 4:50–68.

FISCHER, H. (1933), Sehnsucht und Selbstbefriedigung. Z. psychoanal. Päd., 7:140–144.

—— & PELLER, L. (1934), Eingewöhnungsschwierigkeiten im Kindergarten. Z. psychoanal. Päd., 8:33–36.

FREUD, ANNA (1935), Introductory Notes [to Child Analysis Number]. Psychoanal. Quart., 4:1–2.

—— (1936), The Ego and the Mechanisms of Defense. The Writings of Anna Freud, Volume II. New York: International Universities Press, 1966.

—— (1939–1945), Infants Without Families: Reports on the Hampstead Nurseries. The Writings of Anna Freud, Volume III. New York: International Universities Press, 1973.

—— (1945–1956), Indications for Child Analysis and Other Papers. The Writings of Anna Freud, Volume IV, New York: International Universities Press, 1968.

192 BIBLIOGRAPHY

—— (1956–1965), *Research at the Hampstead Child Therapy Clinic and Other Papers. The Writings of Anna Freud*, Volume V. New York: International Universities Press, 1969.

—— (1965), *Normality and Pathology in Childhood: Assessments of Development. The Writings of Anna Freud*, Volume VI. New York: International Universities Press, 1970.

—— (1966–1970), *Problems of Psychoanalytic Training and the Technique of Therapy. The Writings of Anna Freud*, Volume VII. New York: International Universities Press. 1971.

FREUD, SIGMUND (1900), The Interpretation of Dreams, *Standard Edition*, 3 & 4.*

—— (1905), Three Essays on the Theory of Sexuality. *Standard Edition*, 7:125–243.

—— (1909), Analysis of a Phobia in a Five-Year-Old Boy. *Standard Edition*, 10:3–149.

—— (1919), 'A Child Is Being Beaten': A Contribution to the Study of the Origin of Sexual Perversions. *Standard Edition*, 17:175–204.

FRIES, M. E. (1932), Play Technique in the Analysis of Young Children. *Psychoanal. Rev.*, 14:233–245.

FUCHS, H. (1932), Psychoanalytische Heilpädagogik im Kindergarten. *Z. psychoanal. Päd.*, 6:349–391.

—— (1933), Probleme der heilpädagogischen Kindergartengruppen. *Z. psychoanal. Päd.*, 7:243–250.

GELEERD, E. R. (1943), The Analysis of a Case of Compulsive Masturbation in a Child. *Psychoanal. Quart.*, 12:520–540.

HOFFER, W. (1935), Bericht über die Einleitung einer Kinderanalyse. *Z. psychoanal. Päd.*, 9:271–292.

KATAN [ANGEL], A. (1935), From the Analysis of a Bedwetter. *Psychoanal. Quart.*, 4:120–134.

* *The Standard Edition of the Complete Psychological Works of Sigmund Freud*, 24 Volumes, translated and edited by James Strachey. London: Hogarth Press and the Institute of Psycho-Analysis, 1953–

KLEIN, M. (1923), Infant Analysis. In: *Contributions to Psycho-Analysis*. London: Hogarth Press, 1948, pp. 87–116.

—— (1926), The Psychological Principles of Infant Analysis. In: *Contributions to Psycho-Analysis*. London: Hogarth Press, 1948, pp. 140–151.

—— (1932), *The Psycho-Analysis of Children*. London: Hogarth Press.

KRIS, M. (1932), Ein Märchenstoff in einer Kinderanalyse. Z. *psychoanal. Päd.*, 6:437–441.

LANDAU, A. (1936), Angsterlebnisse eines Dreijährigen. Z. *psychoanal. Päd.*, 10:366–378.

LEVY, E. (1932), Psychoanalytic Treatment of a Child with a Stealing Compulsion. *Amer. J. Orthopsychiat.*, 4:1–23, 1934.

LEVY, K. (1934), Vom Bettnässen des Kindes. Z. *psychoanal. Päd.*, 8:178–195.

MAENCHEN, A. (1936), Denkhemmung und Aggression aus Kastrationsangst. Z. *psychoanal. Päd.*, 10:276–299.

MINOR ZARUBA, E. (1937), Die fünfjährige Nora im Kindergarten. Z. *psychoanal. Päd.*, 11:253–261.

PENSIMUS, K. (1933), Folgen der Entrechtung. Z. *psychoanal. Päd.*, 7:233–242.

—— (1935), A Rejected Child. *Psychoanal. Quart.*, 4:37–49.

PLANK SPIRA, E. (1937), Eine Einschlafstörung aus Todesangst. Z. *psychoanal. Päd.*, 11:44–53.

PÖRTL, A. (1933), Verspätete Reinlichkeitsgewöhnung. Z. *psychoanal. Päd.*, 7:224–232.

—— (1935), Profound Disturbances in the Nutritional and Excretory Habits of a Four-and-One-Half-Year-Old Boy: Their Analytic Treatment in a School Setting. *Psychoanal. Quart.*, 4:25–36.

REDL, F. (1934a), Zum Begriff der "Lernstörung." Z. *psychoanal. Päd.*, 8:155–177.

—— (1934b), Gedanken über die Wirkung einer Phimoseoperation. Z. *psychoanal. Päd.*, 8:319–349.

——— (1935), Der Mechanismus der Strafwirkung. Z. *psychoanal. Päd.*, 9:221–270.

SCHMAUS, M. (1933), Bravheit und neurotische Hemmung. Z. *psychoanal. Päd.*, 7:129–139.

STERBA, E. (1933a), An Abnormal Child. *Psychoanal. Quart.*, 5:375–414, 560–600, 1936.

——— (1933b), Excerpt from the Analysis of a Dog Phobia. *Psychoanal. Quart.*, 4:135–160, 1935.

——— (1934a), Aus der Analyse eines Zweijährigen. Z. *psychoanal. Päd.*, 8:37–72.

——— (1934b), Verbot und Aufforderung, Z. *psychoanal. Päd.*, 8:399–402.

——— (1935), Ein Fall von Essstörung. Z. *psychoanal. Päd.*, 9:99–105.

——— (1936a), Zwei Arten der Abwehr. Z. *psychoanal. Päd.*, 10:263–268.

——— (1936b), Schule und Erziehungsberatung. Z. *psychoanal. Päd.*, 10:141–201.

SYMPOSIUM (1927), On Child Analysis. *Int. J. Psycho-Anal.*, 8:339–380.

WAELDER HALL, J. (1935), Analyse eines Falles von Pavor Nocturnus. Z. *psychoanal. Päd.*, 9:5–70.

WULFF, M. (1927a), A Phobia in a Child of Eighteen Months. *Int. J. Psycho-Anal.*, 9:354–359, 1928.

——— (1927b), Phobie bei einem anderthalbjährigen Kinde. *Int. Z. Psychoanal.*, 13:290–293.

Index

The Writings of Anna Freud

Abbreviated Contents

VOLUME I (1922–1935)

INTRODUCTION TO PSYCHOANALYSIS: LECTURES FOR CHILD ANALYSTS AND TEACHERS

VOLUME II (1936)

THE EGO AND THE MECHANISMS OF DEFENSE

(Revised Edition)

VOLUME III (1939–1945)

INFANTS WITHOUT FAMILIES: REPORTS ON THE HAMPSTEAD NURSERIES

(With Dorothy Burlingham)

Part I: 56 Monthly Reports (February 1941–December 1945)

Part II: Infants Without Families: The Case for and against Residential Nurseries

VOLUME IV (1945–1956)

INDICATIONS FOR CHILD ANALYSIS AND OTHER PAPERS

Part III

Reviews, prefaces, outlines, obituaries

VOLUME V (1956–1965)

RESEARCH AT THE HAMPSTEAD
CHILD-THERAPY CLINIC AND OTHER PAPERS

Part I

Research Projects of the Hampstead Clinic
Assessment of Pathology in Childhood
The Adult Profile
Psychoanalysis and Family Law
Services for Underprivileged Children

Part II

The Contribution of Direct Child Observation to
    Psychoanalysis
Child Observation and Prediction of Development
Adolescence
The Theory of the Parent-Infant Relationship
Links between Hartmann's Ego Psychology and the
    Child Analyst's Thinking
Comments on Psychic Trauma
Obsessional Neurosis

Part III

The Child Guidance Clinic as a Center of Prophylaxis and
    Enlightenment

The Assessment of Borderline Cases
Entrance into Nursery School
Interactions between Nursery School and Child Guidance
    Clinic
Answering Pediatricians' Questions
The Role of Regression in Mental Development
Children in the Hospital
Three Contributions to a Seminar on Family Law
Psychoanalytic Knowledge and its Application to Children's
    Services

Part IV

Prefaces and tributes

VOLUME VI (1965)
NORMALITY AND PATHOLOGY IN CHILDHOOD: ASSESSMENTS OF DEVELOPMENT

VOLUME VII (1966–1970)
PROBLEMS OF PSYCHOANALYTIC TRAINING, DIAGNOSIS, AND THE TECHNIQUE OF THERAPY

Part I

Problems of Termination in Child Analysis
A Discussion with René Spitz
Adolescence as a Developmental Disturbance
A Short History of Child Analysis